Do Llamas Fall in Love?

"An array of puzzling philosophical questions, written with verve, clarity, and wit. Highly recommended."

A.W. Moore – Professor of Philosophy, University of Oxford, and author of *The Infinite*

"Highly entertaining and thought-provoking. Peter Cave is always worth reading!"

Stephen Law – Author of *The Philosophy Gym* and editor of *Think*

"Every point is made with a quip, but behind the badinage lies a wealth of learning and a talent for making things clear."

David Papineau – Professor of Philosophy of Science, King's College, London

"A first-class package of puzzles, stamped with humour and handled with flair."

Laurence Goldstein – Professor of Philosophy, University of Kent

"If llamas can fall in love with philosophy, this witty, clear, entertaining and learned little book is just the thing to make them."

Tim Chappell – Professor of Philosophy, The Open University

About the Author

Writer and broadcaster Peter Cave lectures in philosophy for The Open University. He chairs the Humanist Philosophers of Great Britain and is often in debates, talking about paradoxes, and arguing for good reasoning, especially in ethical, political and religious life. He frequently contributes to philosophy journals and magazines from the academic to the popular, gives talks on philosophy both here and abroad, and introduced BBC radio listeners to a paradoxical fair of fun. Philosophy and reflection, he feels, are often helped when enlivened with tales, images, and the occasional touch of humour. He lives in Soho, London.

Do Llamas
Fall in Love?

33 Perplexing Philosophy Puzzles

Peter Cave

ONEWORLD

OXFORD

A Oneworld Book

Published by Oneworld Publications 2010

Copyright © Peter Cave 2010

The moral right of Peter Cave to be identified as the
Author of this work has been asserted by him
in accordance with the Copyright,
Designs and Patents Act 1988

ISBN 978–1–85168–767–1

Typeset by Glyph International, Bangalore India
Cover design by vaguelymemorable.com
Printed and bound in Great Britain by CPI Cox & Wyman

Cover illustrations by Scott Garrett
Cartoons inside the book © www.fordcartoon.com

Oneworld Publications
UK: 185 Banbury Road Oxford OX2 7AR, England
US: 38 Greene St, 4th Floor, New York, NY 10013, USA

Learn more about Oneworld. Join our mailing list to
find out about our latest titles and special offers at:

www.oneworld-publications.com

CONTENTS

Dedicated to all those who forever lack dedications

PREFACE

Philosophy is the disease of which it is the cure.

If you puzzle and reflect on why, or whether, there are some things you ought or ought not to do – some things that are good; some things bad – then you are something of a philosopher. If you wonder how things really are – whether the mind is nothing but the brain; whether the world is divinely caused – you are something of a philosopher. And if you sometimes raise puzzling questions such as 'What does it all mean?' and 'What's the point?', there is yet more evidence of your living within the philosophers' realm.

Philosophers argue and debate, weave and stumble, and then clarify, within these three realms: of how things ought to be; how things are; and how there is meaning. There is a fourth, concerning knowledge acquisition: the puzzle of how (and if) we can have knowledge of those matters within the three other realms. That gives rise to a fifth, logic, concerning how to reason and argue well about all matters.

This book contains puzzling questions within the five areas mentioned above. The puzzles and perplexities, including some formal paradoxes, range from anguishes of morality and our understanding of the arts, of democracy and religion – to paradoxes of language, logic and love – to rationality and how best to conduct researches zoological. Yes, I managed an 'A to Z' in that sentence.

The puzzles, tales and little dialogues are designed to make us think about deep matters with which we live day by day. Philosophy may have the image of being distant, abstract and out of this world; but the subject does not have to be like that – and often it is not. Thus, the perplexities here often engage an everyday context, sometimes touched with humour. Philosophy can be fun; it can also be addictive. Philosophy reflects on some of our most basic understandings about the world and ourselves, and seeks to expose misunderstandings. Let me, in this Preface, by way of a few tales, draw attention to how some misunderstandings may occur.

'Moore, do you always speak the truth?'

Two of the most eminent philosophers of the early twentieth century were the Cambridge philosophers, Bertrand Russell and G. E. Moore. Moore was perceived as a man of complete honesty and integrity. Russell was worldly wise, a lover of many women – and mischievous. One day, Russell naughtily asked Moore if he always spoke the truth. Moore, being suitably modest, replied 'No'. What should we conclude?

Moore's answer amounted to, 'I do not always speak the truth.' Let us assume, though, that Moore was indeed being modest and everything else Moore ever said was true. Moore's answer now amounts to, 'What I am saying now is not true.' But that is baffling for if what he is saying is not true, then, as that is what he is saying, it is after all true. Moreover, if it is true, it is not true. And that is a contradiction. We meet related paradoxes – and some modesty – in Chapters 6 and 15.

A statement is self-contradictory when there is no way in which it can be true. There is no way it can be true that this sentence is both written in English and not in English. Two statements contradict each other, when if one is true, the other must be false; and if one is false, the other must be true. Philosophers seek consistency, the avoidance of contradictions and other inconsistencies.

Inconsistencies do not exist 'out there' in nature. They arise when we represent, think or speak of the world and find ourselves entangled, as we did when reflecting on Moore's reply to Russell. Philosophical reflection reveals many tangles in our assumptions and ways of living – that is, so to speak, the philosophical disease. Philosophical reflection guides us out of the tangled darkness into the light: well, that is the hope – and the hoped-for cure.

'He could teach me nothing'

Arguably the greatest twentieth-century philosopher is Ludwig Wittgenstein. When he first arrived in Cambridge, where he was quickly seen as a tormented arrogant genius, Russell (yes, the same Russell as above) told him to learn some logic from W. E. Johnson, the established logician. They survived only one session together. Afterwards, Wittgenstein reported back to Russell, 'He could teach me nothing.' Johnson reported back to friends, 'I could teach him nothing.'

Johnson and Wittgenstein, in a sense, were both saying the same thing about Johnson; but they meant very different things. Johnson perceived the young Wittgenstein as conceited and unprepared to listen. Wittgenstein thought of Johnson as fuddy-duddy, out of date. Later, in fact, they became close friends, with Wittgenstein admiring Johnson's piano-playing – radically more so than ever he did Johnson's logic.

The story reminds us that we need to pay careful attention to meaning – to what is intended by a statement – and this requires attention to context, motives and presuppositions. If I say that I saw the Prime Minister on television last night, adding that he was sober, my words alone do not logically imply that he is usually intoxicated; but, given the context and presuppositions, frequent intoxication is conveyed – it is the 'conversational implicature' of what I said.

Casimir Lewy, a philosopher who attended Moore's and Wittgenstein's lectures, was once asked his view of a colleague's recent book. 'It's printed on fine quality paper,' came his heavily Polish-accented response. Nothing more needed to be said. Mind you, when the incident was more recently related, the hearer asked, 'So, what *did* Lewy think of the book?' The wise reply was, 'I think that I've just told you.'

Wittgenstein famously and controversially said, 'Philosophy is the battle against the bewitchment of our intelligence by means of language.' Well, many philosophers strongly reject the idea that philosophical puzzles are just linguistic matters – see what you think as you read on – but all would agree that linguistic care is much needed.

'Bring your washing here' *and* 'fruit or nut'

Søren Kierkegaard, a nineteenth-century Danish philosopher, now seen as a religious existentialist, saw a shop with the sign 'Bring your washing here'. Kierkegaard hurried back to his lodgings, collected his dirty washing and took it to the shop – only to discover that the shop was not a laundry, but a shop that sold shop-signs. The tale reminds us that we need to be careful in assessing what a sign is a sign of. Where signs are displayed is important for correct interpretation of the signs; and matters of interpretation come especially to the fore when we consider questions of how we ought to behave.

I spoke of the world 'out there' in nature as containing no paradoxes, no inconsistencies. The problems arise with our reflections on the world – not with the world. However, the world of morality, of how we should live, of what we ought to do, arguably contains puzzling inconsistencies within it: the inconsistencies do not result solely from inadequate reflections on that world.

The world cannot be such that Liam is both someone who drinks wine and someone who never drinks wine. That is contradictory. However, the moral world, it seems, can be such that Liam both ought to keep his promise and ought not to keep his promise. He ought to keep his promise to see Hedwig otherwise Hedwig will be upset – and he ought not to upset Hedwig. Yet he ought not to keep his promise to see Hedwig because if he does, he upsets Maria and he ought not to upset Maria. Morality and, indeed, our political life raise such dilemmas, as seen, for example, in Chapters 1, 3, 20 and 28.

There are also questions of the objectivity of moral truths. If something is true, there must be something about the world that makes it true: a truth-maker. Well, so it may seem; yet if we hold to that assumption and also accept the existence of moral truths, we need some moral truth-makers in the world. Such truth-makers, as Chapter 22 briefly muses, may seem peculiar.

Here is a non-moral 'fruit or nut' case, courtesy of Elizabeth Anscombe: she presented it many years ago in a philosophy seminar, having encountered a chocolate with a wrapper which read 'fruit or nut'. Now, she reflected, a chocolate can be fruit chocolate; it can be nut chocolate; it can be chocolate that is fruit *and* nut. But what is there about the world that could make it 'fruit *or* nut'? What is the truth-maker for the proposition that the chocolate is fruit or nut? Bafflement about truth-makers, as 'fruit or nut' shows, does not arise solely with regard to moral truths.

Philosophizing: the battle against bewitchment

The central subject matter of philosophy is what we all encounter in everyday life: our experiences, our beliefs about the world, about ourselves and our treatment of others – and those anguishes when, in the night's stillness, we wonder about life's meaning. Philosophers rarely become directly involved in physical experiments, treks through muddy swamps, or the hard work of archaeological digs. We prefer the armchair, pen and paper (well, keyboard), and even the glass of wine. Philosophers do, though, reflect on others' worldly investigations, be they physical, psychological or religious. See, for example, Chapter 18.

Philosophers are curious – prepared to delve into anybody's subject. Bearing in mind that curiosity killed the cat, were philosophers cats they would not last long. As Wittgenstein wrote, 'The philosopher is not a citizen of any community of ideas. That is what makes him into a philosopher.' Philosophers are not bound to one sole area of reflection.

Philosophers use their reason. After all, if you are wondering how you know that you are not dreaming, it is pointless to conduct an experiment, for you may be dreaming that you are conducting the experiment and dreaming the results of the experiment.

Sometimes it is said that there are 'no right or wrong' answers in philosophy. That is wrong. Fallacies in reasoning are spotted; false assumptions are highlighted. Bewitchments are brought to the surface. Having said all that, perplexities usually remain. This contrasts with straight logical or mathematical puzzles where, once things are explained, all is clear. Here is an example of a 'straight puzzle' concerning just the three people mentioned.

> Osbert is in love just with Penelope, but Penelope is in love just with Quentin. Osbert is a philosopher. Quentin is not. Is a philosopher in love with a non-philosopher?

(Is the answer 'Yes', 'No' or 'Cannot tell'? See the notes for the answer.)

Philosophers often present the world, the problems, in differing lights. The lights can illuminate, yet generate further puzzles. Here is an illumination – well, an illuminating challenge.

Nietzsche hypothesized the eternal recurrence – 'the greatest weight' he said – asking whether we could be so well disposed to our lives that we would welcome them being repeated eternally, exactly the same each time round. Of course, were the repetitions exactly the same, with the whole universe repeating itself in the same way, then we should be unaware of the repetitions. We may even doubt the sense of such repetitions. Arguably, though, the eternal recurrence – this most dreadful and anguishing of thoughts – is a picture intended to concentrate our minds on how we should live, on what sort of life we value, and what we can bear: see Chapters 32 and 33.

∨

The philosopher, it has been quipped, is like a blind man in a dark room searching for a black cat – that isn't there. Well, as you dip into these puzzles, sometimes there is feline discovery – and sometimes not. Sometimes the philosophical disease persists; sometimes the cure quells. In either case, I hope you find that the search is usually fascinating, frequently fun and often enriching. And I hope that always, at the very least, the words 'provoking' and 'thought' will spring to mind. Philosophy may ultimately soothe; but before doing so, it should certainly stir.

ACKNOWLEDGEMENTS

I am indebted to many colleagues and students over many years at The Open University and City University London. More recently – and since the sad demise of philosophy at City University (a university without philosophy: is that possible?) – I have been stimulated by the Monday Club philosophers, initiated by Pelham Dobson, who are very different from members of Monday Club traditional. I also thank participants at Claudio Tamburrini's Recidivism Conference, 2009, at the University of Stockholm.

Useful comments have been provided by Laurence Goldstein, Michael Clark, Adrian Moore, Nick Everitt, Gerard Livingstone, Piers Benn, Sophie Bolat, Carolyn Price, Espée Liff, Richard Norman, Jerry Valberg, Andrew Harvey, Martin Holt and John Shand – and members of the Humanist Philosophers. I appreciate them all – both the individuals and the comments.

For valuable aiding ways over the years, practical and intellectual, many thanks to Angela Joy Harvey. My thanks too to Juliet Mabey, Mike Harpley, Kathleen McCully, Kirsten Summers, and all of Oneworld for encouraging these perplexing ventures philosophic.

Ardon Lyon is the philosopher who has, by far, suffered most in this enterprise – as he did with my previous perplexities. He deserves my greatest gratitude. He has battled through much draft material and has showered me with clarity and insight, followed by confusion and outsight, but then enhanced with greater clarity and greater insight, though sometimes we are unsure which are which – always, though, with meticulous care, much kindness, much humour. He should be writing these books – well, too late for these books, but similar and better.

Peter Cave

1

SOMEONE ELSE WILL ...

Jobs are not easy to come by in Little Rock, out in mid-West America, so imagine how pleased Goodman was when offered employment by the local sheriff. His luck was on the up – or so he thought, until the sheriff said a little more.

'You see,' said the sheriff, 'what we really need is a professional hangman. You're ideal for the job, in view of your skill with ropes and knots and shortly, I hope, nooses.'

Goodman gulped. Yes, he wanted a job – he had a family to support – but unlike so many of Little Rock's citizens, the Little Rockeans, he was opposed to hanging. He was a man of principle, at least on this matter.

'No, I really can't take the job,' stammered Goodman. 'It's a pity, but I'm deeply opposed to the death penalty. It's as simple as that.'

'Look,' replied the sheriff, 'I respect your view – though it's not mine – but if you don't take the job, I'll have to offer the position to someone else. Someone else will do the hanging. So, what have you achieved by your refusal?'

'Steadfastness to principle,' replied Goodman, with a sad expression, wondering how to break the news to his family that he had rejected employment so well-paid.

'That's not much of a principle, if it makes you look so sad,' beamed the sheriff. 'Anyway, what of your other principles – your duties such as feeding and educating your children?'

'I know, I know. Principles clash; but there are some things I cannot bring myself to do. Before and after the hangings,

I'd have nightmares. They'd show me how morally wrong it would be.'

'That's just a psychological problem of yours, Goodman; but your duty is to your family – and, to repeat, if you don't take the job, someone else will get it. Nothing is gained by your standing high and mighty on principle. In fact, between you and me, I really want you for the job as I know that you'd treat those awaiting execution humanely, whereas the other contender for the job, Badman, would taunt the prisoners as well as eventually hanging them pretty painfully. That's another reason for you to accept. Come on – take the job!'

Should Goodman go against his principle and take the executioner's job?

'Someone else will, if I do not' is often an attempted excusing factor both for doing what we think that we ought not to do and for failing to do what we think we ought. For example: a woman has fainted on the railway platform; we are in a rush; 'Well, someone else will look after her,' we reflect, as we dash by.

What should we advise Goodman to do? Looking at the dilemma solely in terms of consequences – outcome – regarding overall benefits, Goodman, it would seem, should accept the sheriff's offer. It would help his family; it would make things not quite so bad for those on death row. Those factors should outweigh his discomfort. He may even feel good about himself, something of a martyr, in overcoming his principle.

True, other factors could be cast into the calculation, factors pointing to the opposite conclusion: for example, Badman may have an even bigger family to support.

So far, our reasoning has been directed at likely consequences. For further example, if Goodman's declining the job would lead others to reconsider their support for the death penalty, aiding its eventual prohibition – and were the prohibition to lead to a more flourishing society – then, still on consequential grounds, Goodman would be right in his refusal. But let us assume that, on straightforward consequential grounds, it would be better for Goodman to accept the sheriff's offer. Could anything still be said in support of Goodman's refusal?

This is where we may focus on what sort of person Goodman wants to be, and how integral his principle is to his life. Could Goodman live with himself, live with his conscience, if he allowed himself – as he sees it – to dirty his hands by being executioner? Perhaps staying faithful to his principle, regardless of overall consequences, carries its own moral weight.

An immediate response is that Goodman, in declining the job, is being selfish, putting his own sense of moral well-being above helping his family. Yet is that a fair riposte? Can morality demand that Goodman sacrifice his integrity? Goodman has to live with himself. Perhaps that factor, though – of what makes for Goodman's flourishing life – could simply be entered into a more nuanced consequentialist calculation, with Goodman's sense of integrity given extra weight.

* * *

The above consequentialist approach to morality rests on a detached perspective, a perspective that stands outside Goodman's particular circumstances. It seeks objectivity, taking into account the effects of the proposed action on Goodman, on the prisoners, on Badman, and so forth. Now, Goodman may picture himself lacking certain attachments – he becomes un-swayed by his wife, blind to images of hanging victims – but his decision and resultant action needs, it seems, the motivational *oomph* of his actual feelings, worries and concerns. One question, then, is whether morality, understood as totally detached, could ever provide that oomph. That apart, morality, it may be argued, demands special regard for certain attachments Goodman has – his loyalties, relationships and what matters to him.

Goodman, in making his choice over the job, is making himself. His motivation may arise from his seeing himself as a man of firm principle against the death penalty, or as a man devoted to his family such that he will sacrifice certain principles for that family. In taking the job, though, he could be accepting himself as a hypocrite or coward, unprepared to uphold his principle.

What moves Goodman, and what should move all of us, are our projects and what we see as giving moral sense to our lives. 'Someone else will, if I do not' should carry little weight when we consider how we ought to live our lives.

Similarly, 'Others do it, so I'll do the same' also ought to carry little weight. Consider how some parents lie about their religious faith or their home address in order to get their children into the better school: 'Well, everybody else does.' Insurance claimants over-claim with similar attempted justification. That others do is not sufficient to shield us from condemnation or praise, for we have still chosen to be that sort of person who does as others do.

Where does this leave us over Goodman and the job offer? Well, we can discuss with Goodman; we can draw attention to factors unnoticed. In the end the decision is his. He has to live with what he decides. He ought not to expect a detached answer which he must follow as a puppet follows the pull of the strings, the puppet being no agent, no person, at all. Of course, he could choose to behave *as if* a puppet; but that also is then his personal choice.

When important dilemmas arise, such as our dilemma for Goodman, there is a lot to be said for D. H. Lawrence's injunction, 'Find your deepest impulse and follow it.' Mind you, reflecting on some people and their deepest impulses, there is also a lot to be said for not recommending such action.

3. THE VIOLINIST: SHOULD YOU UNPLUG?

24. EXEMPTIONS: DOCTORS, CONSCIENCE AND THE NIQAB

33. MINDFUL OF BARBARIANS – WITHIN AND WITHOUT

8. GOING FOR COVER – FROM ARMS DEALING TO CASTING COUCHES

2

PINTER AND ISABELLA: TETHERING THEM DOWN

Certain statues of people are so lifelike that they dance around rather than remaining still and unmoving. In Greek mythology that was so of the statues carved by Daedalus for he was such a fine craftsman. Socrates spoke of how the statues of Daedalus would run away like runaway slaves – a revelation of some social interest – unless they were tethered down.

Let us keep the above thought in mind, when musing upon knowledge.

ᐯ

You are walking along a country lane and Isabella, gazing across the field, notices an animal, and says, 'Ah, there's a donkey grazing in the field.' You mumble a response, uninterested, yet trying to show politeness: 'I didn't know you knew about such farming matters.' You hope that donkey talk will not squeeze out the intended romance of the stroll.

Now, what is needed for Isabella to *know* that a donkey is grazing – or, for that matter, for her state not to be one of knowledge? We are, by the way, assuming that Isabella is speaking sincerely, believes what she says – and indeed speaks the truth. The field really does contain a donkey grazing. In other words, Isabella has a true belief; but do true beliefs count as knowledge? Can we add features to the scenario to show how, perhaps, true belief is not thereby knowledge?

How does knowledge differ from true belief?

Why is knowledge more important than true belief?

Isabella gazes at an animal. Now, the animal, in fact, is not a donkey but a goat. Yet Isabella speaks the truth in saying that the field contains a donkey because, unbeknownst to her, a donkey lurks in the corner out of eyesight. Isabella has got things right – but by luck. She lacks knowledge of there being a donkey. She takes a goat to be a donkey.

This may suggest that, for Isabella to *know* that there is a donkey, the donkey needs to feature in the explanation of why she spoke as she did. If we ask her though, she would justify her donkey claim by pointing at a goat – hardly a good justification. Her mistaken thought about the creature that she sees explains why she says that there is a donkey; but the actual donkey in the field has nothing to do with her thought that there is a donkey. She pays no attention to the donkey.

Now, to bring out a further point, let us consider the following scenario, a true one concerning Harold Pinter.

Pinter was lunching at the House of Lords, at the invitation of his father-in-law, Lord Longford. Various lords and dukes chatted to Pinter. A Hackney lad, son of a Jewish tailor, Pinter had grown up in London's East End and had made good as a playwright. 'And do you know the port you're drinking?' asked a Lord Donaldson. 'Dão 1963,' came Pinter's reply, although he had neither seen the bottle nor been told. The waiter was called over. He confirmed Dão 1963. The lords were suitably impressed by Pinter's knowledge: he may be just a playwright, but he's a good judge of port.

Pinter, in our example, paid attention to the port. He was not tasting some other port and mistaking it for Dão 1963. He tasted some port that was Dão 1963; but, as he later confessed, Dão 1963 was the only port he knew. Whichever port he tasted, he would give the Dão 1963 answer. Pinter hit lucky, as did Isabella.

The brief tales of Isabella and Pinter show two different ways in which we may reach the truth by means of good luck, and hence not possess knowledge.

Perhaps knowledge is grander than true belief in that it needs the belief to be appropriately linked to what makes the belief true. The true belief needs to be tethered down, to use Socrates' metaphor at this chapter's very beginning.

The tethering down could be by means of the knowing individuals being able to give good reasons for what they claim – or by there being appropriate external links, causes, between what is believed and what makes the beliefs true.

* * *

Let us now consider Isabella in a different scenario. She first really does see the donkey (and not the goat) and as a result says, 'There's a donkey.' So, what she sees – the donkey – is involved in the explanation of why she believes that there is one. There is an appropriate causal link between what she believes and what makes her belief true. The donkey features in the story about how she came to have certain visual sensations that led to her belief. Indeed, Isabella can justify what she believes. She can truthfully say, 'I can see a donkey right there,' pointing at the donkey.

Does our Isabella, in this scenario, now know that there is a donkey in front of her? Well, it is true that there is one; and she thinks that there is one – and the donkey figures in why she has her belief. Let us, though, have Isabella looking round more intently. She now sees the goat and says, perfectly seriously, 'Ah, another donkey.' Suppose she walks on, turns a corner and exclaims, 'There's another donkey,' but she is now looking at a sheep. She hit lucky with the first case – of seeing the donkey and getting it right – for clearly and surprisingly she cannot distinguish between donkeys, goats and sheep.

The interesting outcome here is that even if Isabella does not walk on and so does not make mistaken comments about goats and sheep, she still lacks knowledge in the first place concerning the donkey. This is because of the following truth, namely: were she to be asked about these other creatures, goats and sheep, she would announce that they too are donkeys. She is unable to discriminate between such creatures – just as Pinter was unable to discriminate between ports. She is liable to make mistakes about such creaturely matters.

*   *   *

Isabella and Pinter, in our tales, lack knowledge because their beliefs about the relevant matters are unreliable. Pinter is no reliable guide, if asked to judge port vintages. Isabella clearly is not to be trusted: if you order a donkey from her, you may end up with a goat or sheep.

Knowledge requires that those who know can be relied upon about the matters in question: they need to be reliably right, though not infallibly so. It is the 'reliably right' feature that makes knowledge so valuable. Were infallibility demanded, knowledge would become a will-o'-the-wisp. Knowledge of my friend Pelham, here and now, does not require my possessing the ability to distinguish him from a fake Pelham, were we to imagine such existed – or from a twin, were such to be shipped over from another land.

A good guide knows how to find the right path; a port connoisseur knows how to distinguish between vintage 1963 and '73; and Isabella, if knowledgeable about animals, should at least be able to sort out the sheep from the goats – and from the donkeys.

3

THE VIOLINIST: SHOULD YOU UNPLUG?

You wake up one mundane Monday, only to discover that this Monday is far from mundane. A tube runs from your body to an unknown man a few feet away. A violinist, it transpires, is plugged into your lymphatic system.

Although bizarre, the tale possesses considerable relevance to the everyday. Before we bring the tale down to earth, let us fly this phantasy.

How did the violinist come to be plugged into you? Well, maybe you were in hospital for some minor tests. While you slept, the violinist, unconscious, was rushed into the ward. The doctors knew that the only way to save him was to plug his system into yours. Fortunately for the violinist, and unfortunately for you, your lymphatic system possesses a rare property, one essential for maintaining the violinist's life. The violinist's use of your system does not endanger your health;

but, while plugged, your life is somewhat inconvenienced. The violinist will go everywhere with you – which could well give rise to embarrassments in your social, personal and romantic life.

Right now, the violinist is sitting by your bedside. He is fine, so long as he remains plugged. You flick the tubing connecting his body to yours. He is well aware that you could simply disconnect it. All would then be well with you; all not well with him. He would die, perhaps a horrible death. He needs you in order to live.

Understandably, the violinist begs you not to unplug him. It is life or death for him – of convenience or the opposite for you. Yet there are other factors. He has no right to use of your body – or does he? He surely has a right to life. By unplugging him, would you not be violating that right? You would certainly be causing him to die.

Are you within your rights to unplug the violinist?

One line leads to the answer 'Yes'. You granted him no right to your body. No agreement was made. He is, so to speak, trespassing on your body; so, you are well within your rights to remove him. True, he would die as a result of the removal, but that is neither your intent nor your fault. It is an unfortunate consequence of you asserting your rights. If, miraculously, he were to survive, you should have no objection; presumably you would feel relieved. In unplugging him, your aim is not to kill him.

We may feel queasy with the above response. Are you not violating his right to life, by insisting on the higher priority of your right to be un-trespassed upon? Suppose he merely needs use of your body for one day, until some drugs arrive. Would you still be within your rights to insist on unplugging?

The thoughts above raise two fundamental questions. One question concerns what is involved in possessing a right. Another question concerns morality's extent.

On the first question, people speak readily of everyone having a right to life. People do not speak so readily of everyone having a right to whatever is required for life. The violinist has a right to life. He requires use of your body, but he does not have a right to that use. Millions of people suffer from malnutrition and disease that will kill them; they have a right to life. Do they therefore have a right to assistance from you – for example, by your giving to relevant charities? Someone needs a kidney transplant. Does he have a right to your kidney? After all, you only need one. We spend considerable money on luxuries: we assume a right to spend our money as we wish; we assume that our right outweighs the requirements of others, those with the right to life, for maintenance of their lives.

'Rights' talk is cheap: what is costly is providing means for people to exercise their rights. Possessing the right to life counts for little if it fails to carry any duty on others to enable that right to be fulfilled. 'Tis small comfort to the starving to know that they have a right to life, but no right to the excess food that we keep for ourselves.

Before offering more thoughts about rights, let us turn to the second question, namely, of morality's extent. Even if you would not be violating the violinist's rights by unplugging him – the result being his death – would you not still be doing something wrong, if you did unplug? Morality embraces not only rights, but also qualities such as honesty, loyalty, kindness, courage and forgiveness. In our violinist tale, it would surely be cruel to insist on your rights straight away. If the violinist needed use of your body for just a few hours or even weeks, would not granting him that use be the decent thing to do?

Of course, there are degrees and degrees. It would be extraordinarily kind of you, to accept the violinist attached for the rest of your life. Surely, morality does not demand such exceptional self-sacrifice. In that sort of case, maybe the violinist should recognize the unfair burden he would be putting on your life, and take the courageous path of sacrificing himself. Recall Captain Oates in Scott's disastrous South Pole venture of 1912. In order to avoid being a burden, Oates crawled out of the tent into the blizzards with the famous words, 'I am just going outside and may be some time.' No one had a right to demand that sacrifice, yet maybe Oates did the right thing – despite its ultimate futility.

The violinist, Captain Oates and many other examples remind us that moral dilemmas do not all reduce to conflicting 'rights'. Moral dilemmas can be fed from many quarters and the feeding makes morality something of a mess. You may, for example, think that a lot hangs on the value of the violinist – to himself, but also to society. Were the violinist a lousy player and a depressed drug addict, you may feel far less inclined to allow him use of your body than you would were he a famous violinist of impressive skills. Think how your attitude would change, depending whether the violinist was also a burglar and wife-beater, or a surgeon capable of saving many lives. Yet should the morality of which lives we save hang on the value of those lives to the community?

*   *   *

Rights range from the most trivial – I could give you rights over my laptop – to radically important ones concerning life and death. The United Nations seems to have uncovered a vast range of rights, taking us from the right to life to the right to maternity leave. This shows the danger of how, without care, 'rights' talk becomes devalued. Certain basic moral principles, it seems, justify talk of moral rights. We typically accept that it is wrong to kill another human being; and it is that which immediately grounds the 'right to life'. In contrast, lots of reasoning would be needed to justify maternity leave as a significant 'right'.

Accepting that 'rights' talk highlights certain moral principles as fundamental – trump cards to be played, when in moral dilemmas – the question remains of the source of those principles (a puzzle for Chapter 22). Some philosophers have argued that there are 'natural' rights, rights built within nature, maybe courtesy of God, maybe of our human nature. Jeremy Bentham, an early nineteenth-century thinker, came up with the wonderful quip that such talk is 'nonsense on stilts'. Yet Bentham embraces the utilitarian principle that we ought to seek the greatest happiness of the greatest number. Now, is that principle mysteniously built into nature? Is it standing on nature's stilts, though not God's, as nonsense?

Suppose keeping the violinist alive, plugged into you for years and years, would maximize overall happiness. We should surely still doubt whether morality could demand that you sacrifice yourself in that way – however well the violinist played.

24. EXEMPTIONS: DOCTORS, CONSCIENCE AND THE NIQAB

22. THE FROG, THE SCORPION AND 'THOU SHALT NOT'

28. ON HOW GOOD PUNISHMENT IS BAD, SO BAD

20. MISFORTUNE, MISS FORTUNA – AND MALICIOUS DELIGHT

4

RESOLUTIONS, GOOD INTENTIONS – AND CREAM BUNS

When Jane eats the big cream bun, her New Year's good intentions to stick to her dietary plan now have a bun-sized flaw. She knows that the planned diet is best for her health, but she is weak when faced with cream and bun. She has shown weakness of will. She is weak-willed.

Actions, though, speak louder than words – or so it is said. And Jane's bun-clasping action must surely mean that, at the clasp, her belief was that, all things considered, one bun would do no significant harm. She must have judged that, taking everything into account, the bun-eating was the best thing, right then, for her to do. If she did not so judge, she would not have chosen to succumb to temptation.

Paradoxically, though, the thought that actions speak louder than words can rule out weakness of will, even its possibility. Whatever we do, when acting freely, manifests what we take to be for the best, all things considered – or,

as Socrates argued over two thousand years ago, 'No one willingly and knowingly does what is wrong.' Obviously, we may make mistakes about what is best; but we always do, given the circumstances, what we take to be best. Well, that is the idea.

True, Jane sincerely believed that she needed to lose weight for the sake of her health; true, she wanted to be slim; true, she was well aware that big cream buns would not assist that project. But pressed against those considerations were her desire for the immediate cream-filled pleasure and her belief that one bun would not undermine her dieting project. So, all things considered, bearing in mind her desires and beliefs, she was surely acting rationally, and displaying no weakness of will at all. Yet is that right? Can weakness of will be shown so easily to be illusory?

We ask that question for our everyday experience tells us that we often do suffer from weakness of will. We may seriously intend to study all evening for the examination the next morning, yet instead we meet up with friends and watch the snooker. We know we ought not to have a drink as we shall be driving; but we soon find ourselves with drink in hand and in mouth. Yet, if weakness of will genuinely occurs, what moves people, if not their intentions based on their beliefs and desires? If weakness of will does not occur, what is the right explanation of those cases that seem to be instances of the will's weakness?

How is weakness of will possible?

Cases of weakness of will – or what are taken to be such – differ from cases where the individuals concerned act under compulsion. If Jane is force-fed a bun, that clearly does not manifest weakness of will on her part. It is not weak will, if Jane suffers from a compulsive disorder with no chance of resisting the buns. Cases of weak will are ones in which, it seems, the individuals could resist whatever should be resisted – the gluttony, the lust, the sloth – yet they do not.

Returning to Jane as weak-willed, the following could surely be true. She truly wants to keep strictly to the diet; she recognizes that one bun now could easily pop her on the slippery slope to many more. Further, she sincerely values the project of dieting. And yet she still chooses to eat of the bun and savour the cream. She fails to act on her belief and desire concerning the diet: she acts against her better judgement. She could have exercised self-control, yet did not. That is weakness of will *par excellence*. It is sometimes known as 'akrasia': *kratos* being Greek for power, the *a* negating the power. It is also known, somewhat unattractively, as 'incontinence'.

Jane's actions, say many philosophers, cannot be explained, if they do not issue from her beliefs and desires. If so, we may be led to a revised understanding – the revisionary approach – of what Jane is truly committed to, when finally choosing the bun.

The Socratic approach, for example, is that the sight of the bun leads Jane to become, metaphorically, short-sighted: she is unable to see the future value of health clearly enough; it is too distant. The value of future good health appears small compared with the value of the immediate creamy pleasure; so, whatever Jane is saying about her dieting commitment, her current genuine belief is that eating this bun right now is better overall than resistance.

Another suggestion, in that spirit, is that although Jane genuinely believes that sticking to the diet is valuable, it is conditional, depending on circumstances. In these very circumstances, of the bun immediately before her, she now believes it is better to eat than not. Of course, later on she may well regret yielding to the bun-shaped temptation.

There is a simple challenge to the type of approach above. Except for trying to explain away weak will as illusory, why must we hold that Jane believes bun-eating on this occasion is better than not? True, she *may* believe that 'just one bun' does not matter; but she may insist that she knows that she ought not to be eating even the one: that may be her sincere belief. The man who takes another drink before driving off may believe that the risk of accident is worth taking; if so, he is reckless, but not weak-willed. He may, though, have no such belief. His belief may be that he ought not to have the extra drink, yet drink he does. We have all, no doubt, had experiences of such weakness. Evaluative judgements – what we believe best and our resultant intentions – are not always aligned to motivational strength.

Intentions, be they good or bad, do not get things done. Just because I intend to do something, it does not follow that I do it. I need to act on the intention. Weakness of will occurs when I fail to act on my best intentions: hence it is, allegedly, an irrational state for the agent. Quite how best to explain that failure remains obscure. Models are given of the self as divided within – with desires in conflict with reason and duty – but such models raise their own puzzles. With which division of the self do I most readily identify? What or who, indeed, is the 'I' that judges between the conflicting parts?

*　　　*　　　*

We have deliberately left open what is involved in the judgement that something is 'best'. We may judge what is best purely with regard to self-interest; but we may also take into account what we consider to be our duty, of what morality dictates, or, for that matter, of what our commitment to particular causes demands. Weakness of will can be readily seen when the agent recognizes that, for example, she really ought to help the distressed child or denounce some fraudulent behaviour, yet does not. Just as Jane could not stick to what she sincerely thought best for her health – instead she succumbed to the bun – so we often fail to stick to what we sincerely think is the right thing to do, but succumb instead to perceived self-interest. We are weak creatures indeed.

The 'weakness' in 'weakness of will' suggests that it never deserves recommendation. Now, when individuals develop characters so weak that they fail to follow their true intentions, fail to stick to their principles, we tend to lack respect for them. But sometimes it may be best – for others and even for themselves – if they are weakly willed. Would that those who firmly believe in genocide be weak-willed and, instead of being true to their belief, be driven by humanity, compassion and fellow-feeling.

 **1. SOMEONE ELSE WILL ...**

26. PREFERENCES: AVOIDING THE MONEY PUMP

19. ADDICTED TO LOVE

12. WHAT SORT OF CHILDREN SHOULD THERE BE?

5

'BUT IT'S ART, DEAR AUNT MATILDA'

It wasn't my fault. It was Aunt Matilda, my aged aunt, who wanted a trip round the art galleries – but I knew it wouldn't go well. She was disgusted by the sexuality expressed in Eric Gill's sculptures of a diminished Christ on the cross next to a naked and voluptuous woman ('How can that be art?') and when she encountered the explicit homosexual activity displayed in Robert Mapplethorpe's much-praised photography, she was on the verge of calling the police. Further on, she came across some graphic work by Gilbert and George, with spelt-out obscenities, racist terms – and worse, once she understood the materials some artists used. She was shocked.

⩔

Aunt Matilda's responses raise the question of whether, for art, anything goes. Art is for art's sake, it has been said: it should be left to its own devices.

The mere mention of some things can be inept and discourteous. However much you thought the deceased disreputable, it would be inappropriate and unkind to raise the matter with his family at his graveside. When Engels' wife died, it was inconsiderate of Marx, in his condolences, to move quickly into requesting a monetary loan. And when talking to families who have recently lost sons in battle, it would be insensitive to question the value of those battles. Some things ought not to be said or done in certain contexts. Of course, there are other contexts where those same things may be said or done – sometimes rightly so. Perhaps the deceased ought to be exposed; the justifications for war may deserve to be challenged.

The puzzle here is whether artists, 'in the name of art', ought to be allowed to get away with anything, however controversial, obscene or even illegal. Once, in Britain, the Lord Chamberlain would prohibit certain displays and writings, be they in galleries, on stage or in books, and today various dictatorships censor the arts. Even the most tolerant society, of course, requires some censorship – for example, to prevent harm to individuals and oppression of certain groups. There are laws against incitement, and against racist and sexist remarks. Should the arts, though, be exempt from prohibitions, be the prohibitions enshrined in custom, morality or law?

Should the arts be ring-fenced?

The fencing clearly fails in some areas. 'In the name of art' is no justification for real murders, real-life thefts and fraudulent investment activities. Such activities typically remain unjustified, even if performed with artistic intent; even if the knife marks display an aesthetic harmony; the thieves conduct their thievery as a ballet; and the fraud involves some fine writing. Putting such cases to one side, what may we say to Aunt Matilda? Matilda thinks that the artistic expressions – of blasphemies, obscenities, racisms – are being wrongly protected. Is she blinkered, out of touch, reactionary?

One natural reply to Aunt Matilda is that art is concerned with form, with structure, with generating aesthetic awareness:

'art for art's sake' indeed. The content need not be key, but the way the content is expressed. Paintings and literary descriptions of Christ being crucified, of the horrors of war, can yet be beautiful and astonishing works. Onetime censored books, such as Lawrence's *Lady Chatterley's Lover*, are significant works of art because of their form and language. Art, it may be said, does not exist to cause political change; and in practice it is usually confined to a few locations with the hallowed aura of 'art gallery' or 'library'. As for delicate souls who may be offended, well, they need neither enter the gallery nor open the book.

Another natural reply to Aunt Matilda is grounded in opposition to the first reply. Even where art is valued for its form, it is often intended to be provocative – and to effect change. Think of Picasso's *Guernica* which symbolized the Spanish civil war and the horrors of dictatorship. Art may question existing laws and taboos, stimulating social change – often for the better. That is why art, even if racist, obscene or challenging of current beliefs, should be protected.

The second reply rightly recognizes that art sometimes can, does and should stir; but its line of argument is weak. It is weak because, similarly, we could argue that riots are provocative, challenging existing laws sometimes for the better; and that is why riots promoting racism or obscenity merit protection. Perhaps the art and riots analogy, though, can be rebutted. Riots may directly harm others: that is why such disorder is resisted. Art being viewed, opera being listened to, books being read, are more akin to seminars with high-minded discussion. Well, so it may be argued, though not well-argued.

Even orderly demonstrations, with marchers chanting racist beliefs, even public sexual orgies, causing no direct harm, are currently illegal in Britain. Yet when similar racism or sexuality occurs in art galleries – well, it may escape prohibition. Perhaps it is valuable to designate certain public spaces for the currently unacceptable to be displayed, even accepted. Perhaps the arts offer cover for this. Lovers of artistic freedom, though, would be unhappy with that freedom's defence being that it allows people to let off steam.

This brings us to the delicate perplexity of 'What is art?' If we are unable to distinguish art from, for example, racist demonstrations, then if 'anything goes' for art, so 'anything goes' would apply to the demonstrations, whether or not the demonstrators wore tutus and danced the demonstration.

People often pass the buck to galleries' curators to decide what is art – but how do curators decide? Suppose some 'galleries' displayed only paintings, sculptures and films that glorified the Holocaust and Hitler. Assuming no artistic irony, we should be tempted to think that some political headquarters now had a new designation over its entrance. Suppose a new 'gallery' promoted paintings that represented women as inferior to men and eternal heaven to believers who killed non-believers. That could be the means whereby an extreme religious faction sought to promote its ideas. If art is to be allowed a special status, these examples remind us that it is important to determine what counts as art.

*   *   *

Presumably curators ought to exhibit good art. Perhaps the above hypothesized galleries – with works glorifying oppression – would necessarily be exhibiting bad art. Yet even if the art glorifies the morally disreputable, may it not possess aesthetic merit?

When judging a painting, you may be attracted by its tone and colours, yet find the shapes too jarring and jagged for what the painting represents. Indeed the jarring and jagged-ness may be so great that you fail properly to appreciate the tonal harmony. So, too, a painting *could* attract you for its tone and colours, yet because of what it represents – the glorifica-tion of anti-Semitism; the denigration of women – you are repulsed, unable to attend to the aesthetics. It has failed for you. Yet viewers who share the painting's moral stance may value its form as well as the feelings that it arouses. Mind you, the commitment to what it promotes may be so highly valued and stimulating that such viewers lose sight of the painting's aesthetic value.

The above considerations have not helped us to identify a line between acceptable and unacceptable art, and that is probably because there is no line to find. We need to muddle through, putting up with a lot of questionable art, calling in the authorities only when some serious incitement to harm is likely to occur. We may, though, ask ourselves how *we* should respond to works of art promoting the obscene or morally disreputable. How do you think you would react?'

If your truthful answer, in particular cases, is 'with repulsion', then that may show you are a decent sort of person. It may, though, also show a failure on your part to separate out aesthetic value from moral value. It may show a failure to recognize that one may be both attracted to, and repulsed by, one and the same work – attracted, for example, by the form and execution; repulsed by content and purpose. When lacking such failures, you may be keen to own the controversial paintings for their aesthetics. Yet choosing to hang pictures glorifying genocide and slavery, with racist and obscene language, in your home – well, however fine the form and execution of the paint, does that not say something about you that you would not want said?

24. EXEMPTIONS: DOCTORS, CONSCIENCE AND THE NIQAB

22. THE FROG, THE SCORPION AND 'THOU SHALT NOT'

17. LET THE MUSIC PLAY

6

MODESTY AND SHAME:
A CAT AND MOUSE TALE

'Know thyself,' said the ancient Athenian philosopher Socrates, deriving the injunction from the Delphic Oracle. Many of us would hesitate to obey, from fear of what we may uncover. Yet there are cases where we cannot obey, or so it seems, without losing characteristics that we should be pleased to uncover. And, by coincidence, in a Delphi Taverna, a cat and mouse engaged in a debate that raised precisely such matters.

‌⩔

CLATEO CAT: I bet you wish you were me. Feel my silky coat – yes, I've just won the International Feline Beauty Contest. And did I mention how I received special commendation for my thesis 'Prowling at night: reflections on Socrates'? And in the marathon, I …

MENA MOUSE: Oh dear – *so* immodest, Clateo, with all that boasting. Wouldn't a little modesty become you?

CLATEO: Nothing wrong with immodesty; after all, I merely tell it as it is. No point hiding my light under a bushel – or in a mouse-hole. Follow my example, Mena. True, you're just a grey mouse, but I hear on the grapevine that you have many achievements. The fastest mouse in the house, in the taverna …

MENA: That's nothing – the competition is poor …

CLATEO: Not what I hear, Mena – and there's your Cat-Mouse Reconciliation Project. Also your excellent work with asylum-seeking mice and …

MENA: But that's just what any mouse would do …

CLATEO: Mena, you at least have to admit you're excellent at being modest, don't you know?

MENA: I'm not being modest – just telling it as it is.

*   *   *

Immodest Clateo tells it as it is. He is immodest, given the telling; but he would also be immodest merely in thinking so highly, so proudly, of himself. Clateo knows that he is immodest, but what of Mena Mouse? Mena certainly sounds as if she is modest; and let us assume that she is. Why does she find it difficult to recognize that she is?

Can modest individuals know that they are modest?

We may know that we are kind or mean, courageous or cowardly. We may know that we are conceited, proud and immodest – yet can we know that we are modest? Modesty, here, of course, concerns our achievements, our good features, not our resistance to flaunting the body bared.

To put it paradoxically – the Modesty Paradox – if we know we are modest, then we are not. Modesty requires that we do not overestimate our achievements – but it requires more than that. Clateo Cat may be accurate in the estimate of his achievements, yet is clearly not modest. Modesty, it appears, needs us to underestimate our achievements, diminishing their importance, yet not reflectively and deliberately so. Were we to underestimate deliberately, conscious of that fact, we should be falsely modest: we would be well aware of our achievements, yet pretending they are not that great. That would be a pretence at modesty.

Modest individuals, such as Mena, genuinely see their achievements as less significant than they really are. They see their kindness or generosity, or being the fastest mouse in the house or taverna, as not especially impressive. Paradoxically, modesty – usually taken as a virtue – requires some sincere yet poor evaluation of one's qualities.

Assuming that modest individuals cannot know that they are modest, Mena Mouse could not acknowledge her modesty, saying 'I am modest'. Others, though, could truthfully describe her as modest, as indeed Clateo did. Paradoxically, Clateo can say something true about Mena that Mena cannot say about herself.

The above needs a caveat. Modest individuals may occasionally take a detached attitude about themselves, step out of their skin, and reflect that they have modest tendencies. Even if that is so, that is far removed from, on particular occasions, consciously underplaying what they are. A man – or mouse – who proclaims modesty acts immodestly.

*   *   *

MENA: I forgive your immodesty, Clateo, but I'm not so sure about forgiving you for chasing my little friends the other day. They were really scared. Didn't you feel any shame?

CLATEO: Funny you should ask. Yes, I felt ashamed; but then, being aware of that feeling, I felt rather good about myself – at being the kind of cat who feels bad about his chasing behaviour. That, though, lessened my feeling of shame, so I felt ashamed of that lessening. But then ...

MENA: Don't tell me – you felt good about yourself at being the sort of cat who could feel ashamed about that. I suppose you started feeling bad again as a result and ...

CLATEO: By that stage, I was so befuddled, swaying to and fro from bad to good – well, I slept it all off.

*   *   *

Mena cannot be modest and be aware of her modesty. Now, Clateo was aware of his shame, yet that awareness seemed to undo the full extent of his shame; so we are led to the question:

Can I, if reflective, ever be properly ashamed?

Sensitive individuals, when they wittingly do something bad, should surely feel shame, remorse or regret. Yet in feeling shame, they are not as bad as shameless individuals, individuals who do not care. Once sensitive individuals are aware of this, the paradoxical result is a reduction in their shame – for they are now feeling a little better about themselves.

We need not stop there. Now feeling a little better about themselves, the individuals may feel ashamed of this feeling better, for it detracts from their feeling bad about whatever they did; and, reflecting on this new level of shame, they feel a little better about themselves again. And so on. Whenever feeling better about themselves at feeling ashamed, they move to a new level of shame; but that awareness spirals them into another level of feeling pleased with themselves at being so ashamed.

There is nothing odd in having feelings about feelings. You may feel harassed, and feel irritated with yourself at feeling harassed. You may blush with embarrassment and feel embarrassed at blushing, thus blushing more. There is nothing odd about reflecting on your feelings. In as far as you reflect – human psychology being as it is – you may be distracted from the full immediacy of the feelings upon which you reflect. That is one reason, relied upon by certain therapists, why talking about feelings can reduce your direct involvement in them, thus reducing their intensity. The puzzle of shame, though, does not rest on simple distraction.

Shameful Clateo, on reflection, recognizes that his being ashamed possesses some moral merit. The result is that it is impossible for him to catch the full extent of his badness about which to be ashamed. Although he appears to have a grip on the badness, his reflection on the virtue of his being ashamed leads to a diminution of that badness. That is because he now recognizes that he has the worthy feature of being ashamed. Yet he may be ashamed at how he has, apparently, diminished his badness in that way; thus he spirals.

Clateo cannot know the full continuous extent of his shame; for if he seems to catch it, he loses it. Of course, others may know that he is truly ashamed of his behaviour, and merits some praise for being so – but that is what he cannot know, without destabilizing the shame.

'Know thyself' is all very well, but Socrates might have added that there are some good things about ourselves – being modest, feeling ashamed – upon which it is best not to reflect. Socrates claimed to know only of his ignorance; but in stinging people's complacency with unsettling questions,

Socrates was a philosophical gadfly – arguably a shameless and immodest one, one so good at puncturing the immodesty of others.

23. CREAMY PHILOSOPHERS: WHO KNOWS WHO KNOWS ...

26. PREFERENCES: AVOIDING THE MONEY PUMP

13. THE CARD-SHARP CAMEL *or* 'YOUR NUMBER'S UP'

15. JESTERS, BERTRAND RUSSELL AND PARADOX

7

A BOTTLE IMP – FOR SALE

Allow me to introduce you to Miss Imp. She is a genie of immense power and lives in this bottle in front of you. With a 'Buyer beware' tag yet to be explained, she is, for the first time, on the market, on offer – for sale. Buy her, and she will bring forth everything that you want, be it fame and fortune, sex and success, or just a comfortable life, tending your garden. This is known to be true. Furthermore, her purchase price is any sum you care to name. Miss Imp will give you whatever you want; so, you do not even have to part with the money right now. An IOU is readily accepted. Once you own her, she will conjure up whatever sum you require for payment.

Now, let us face the 'Beware'. The snag, the caveat, is that whoever owns the imp must at some stage, to avoid eternal torment, eternal damnation, sell her for less than he or she paid. Any potential purchasers must be told of this vital condition. Bearing all that in mind, how much would you pay for Miss Imp?

Obviously, you would not pay the lowest unit of money – a penny or a cent. You could never sell her for less than that; and so you would be eternally damned. (We assume that you and others are not otherwise so damned.) Would you buy her for two pennies or two cents? Well, you would then have to sell her, at some point, for one penny or one cent – and a potential purchaser would be crazy to buy her for those sums, for how could the imp ever be sold on?

Of course, you could take a risk – a big risk? – buying her for £1,000, thinking someone would surely take her off your hands for £999, for that someone could think that someone else would be prepared to pay £998 later on. And so on ... But not 'and so on'. If – if – all possible purchasers are rational and farsighted, lacking desire for eternal torment, it looks as if no one would buy Miss Imp, however large the sum.

As with many philosophical paradoxes, we have a tale that, after a little reflection, traps us. Indeed, if anyone currently owns a Miss Imp – why are you looking at me? – he is already trapped.

The tale, you may think, is a crazy tale. Why does it matter? Well, it raises the question of how far ahead it is rational to look. With the Bottle Imp, we casually popped in 'rationality' and 'farsightedness', drawing the conclusion that it would be crazy to buy Miss Imp for even a million pounds. It is crazy because, further down the line, someone would become vividly aware of needing to sell her, impossibly, for one penny or one cent. But is it rational to consider that far ahead?

How much of the future is it rational to take into account?

May it not be rational, in fact, to pay one million pounds for Miss Imp? Remember, you commit to the deal, receive the Imp who then magics the million pounds for you. If it strikes you as rational to buy Miss Imp for one million pounds, presumably someone else may believe it rational to take her off your hands for £999,999. The evidence for that purchaser's belief would be your purchase of Miss Imp for the million pounds: the purchaser would think he could sell her on for £999,998. After all, there is negligible difference between one million pounds and £999,998. Interestingly, what someone considers rational – and what may end up being rational – can be partially determined by what others consider rational. Of course, as we anticipate the trading of Miss Imp for diminishing sums, we become less and less certain whether there would be 'rational' purchasers.

With the Imp, if you are to be a purchaser, you need other people to follow suit. In other cases, you may desire just the opposite. For example, in order to become a priest at the ancient shrine of Nemi, you needed to slay your predecessor. Were you to judge it rational to accede to the priesthood, then, if others sought to follow your example, you would risk meeting with a sticky end.

The Imp makes us wonder how much of the future should influence our actions today. People save up for holidays, but if they saved for another year, they may afford better holidays. Suppose you have a bottle of wine that improves with age: why not wait for another year – and another, and another – before drinking the wine? Of course, we may spot varying degrees of uncertainty, such as risk of bottle breakage; but is such future uncertainty the sole factor that should account for how far we peer?

If you drink the wine after five years, you may regret not waiting until year six, when it would have tasted better. Were the wine to improve indefinitely and were you immortal, you would never drink the wine. Well, you would never drink the wine, if it is irrational to do something that you know you will later regret – and you would regret the wine drinking, if you judge that you should maximize satisfactions. It is, though, that judgement which is mistaken.

Here is a mundane example. People know that faster and cheaper computers become available. If that dominates their thinking, they defer buying a computer – for ever. They are always aware that there will be better deals next year. Searching for the ideal – be it a computer, the best wine, or the finest lover – leads not merely to finding no ideal, but also to lost opportunities of enjoying the pretty good. The tension is, summarily put, between 'good' now and 'better' then.

* * *

Consider a sum of money, say £500, that you could donate to a worthwhile charity right now, saving some people from starvation. That would be good – but maybe deferring the gift would be better. Maybe the returns on the money, if invested, together with likely reductions in costs for nutrition packages, would lead to that money, if donated in the distant future, saving many more lives. If more lives would be saved in that way, ought you not to let people starve now for the greater future good of others? But that 'future' would never come, for the argument, in principle, could be applied again and again.

The examples show that it is often irrational to seek to maximize satisfactions, whatever economists may say. Rationality typically requires us to settle for what is good enough – for 'satisficing'. Regarding ourselves, satisficing may be viewed as manifesting the virtue of moderation over greed. Regarding aid for others, it manifests the virtue of being moved by distressed people *now*, more so than unknown future people.

The distant future weighs heavily for some. Ozone-layer depletion, pollution, nuclear waste: people increasingly worry about future generations. Yet that worry risks diverting resources and attention – based on changeable projections of benefits to future generations – away from real people suffering right now. Further, the concern for benefiting future generations encourages changes in current social policies. Such changes almost certainly mean that individuals born in the future will differ from those who would otherwise have been born. Paradoxically, future individuals have been helped by producing different future individuals – hardly a benefit for those who, as a result, will not exist.

Making sacrifices now for distant future and uncertain benefits, be they for ourselves or for later generations, can be irrational. It is a matter of degree; but as John Maynard Keynes famously quipped, 'In the long run, we're dead.' True, Keynes had no eternal damnation lined up, courtesy of Miss Imp, to build into his calculations. His quip reminds us, though, that we are finite human beings, without perfect foresight, without perfect rationality.

Finite as we are, settling for what comes along that is satisfactory is often more rational than deferring until something better comes along later. And waiting for the best can mean waiting for – well, nothing at all.

12. WHAT SORT OF CHILDREN SHOULD THERE BE? →

13. THE CARD-SHARP CAMEL *or* **'YOUR NUMBER'S UP'** →

32. LIFE WITHOUT END: TOO MUCH OF A GOOD THING? →

8

GOING FOR COVER – FROM ARMS DEALING TO CASTING COUCHES

'Naturally, we have the highest professional standards,' smiled the woman in glasses so dark.

'Of course,' slurred Dan lazily, 'But why are you wining and dining me? Is there a big TV series you're wanting me to front?'

'Media exposure,' said the woman, 'could be a consequence, so easily a consequence, depending on your decision this evening.'

Dan missed the import of those words: he always became distracted when a little tipsy, with nubile waitresses surrounding him.

'Yes, we're aware of your interest in North Korea – and in "helping" pretty girls into the industry. You're an intriguing man, Dan. Our researchers are fascinated with every aspect of your life.'

Dan felt a chill of sobriety. He now paid attention, his cheeks battling between fear-filled whiteness and embarrassed redness.

'But, but … but … now listen here … '

'Don't worry. You did nothing wrong with those armament contracts – and your private investments and little peccadilloes are no one else's business. Is that what you were going to say? I cannot agree more. That's why I invited you along.'

Dan nodded, but sensed relief would be premature.

'Rest assured, Dan, my company is on your side. But some others are not. Newspapers – scurrilous rags – are already offering our company large sums for guidance concerning your life. Politically, you're an important beast. Now, if you would see your way to making us a donation – it would need to be pretty large – we'd ensure the media researchers turn nothing up. We'll give them different prey to chase.'

'And if I cannot afford to make this, er ... er ... donation?'

'Well then, the researchers will just have to do what they have to do. They're just doing their job.'

'But this is blackmail,' Dan exploded.

'Now, now, Dan. Watch your language. See this as a staggering opportunity. And we're hoping society will soon become so enlightened that we can incorporate ourselves as Blackmail plc, our motto being: *we cover your uncover*. Whatever we uncover about lives, we keep them covered from the eyes of others – given suitable donations. A valuable service, I'm sure you agree.'

What's wrong with blackmail?

Blackmail is illegal; it is immoral. So it is said. Why? Blackmailers offer clients – 'Not victims' insists the would-be Blackmail plc – opportunities otherwise lacking. If Blackmail plc just spilled the beans, the blackmailed would indeed be victims; but Blackmail plc provides a valuable choice – between publicity and no publicity. True, there are monetary costs involved with the non-publicity route; but individuals are free to take the public exposure route, making no donations.

Many, though, would prefer making donations, with no exposure.

Let us concentrate on the morality. The two elements to the blackmailer's offer are individually permissible. There is nothing wrong about exposing the truth. There is nothing wrong in asking for donations for one's own benefit. So, it may be argued, having the choice between two moral options must also be moral.

We can swiftly reject that argument. Driving a car is morally permissible, but not if the context includes drinking. Kissing can be highly desirable, but not so desirable if one party has eaten garlic. Laughing is surely innocent enough, but not so innocent at a funeral. The drinking, garlic and funeral attendance are themselves acceptable, but not when combined with driving, kissing and laughing. The combinations lack the acceptability of the parts in isolation – and we can easily explain why. Drink driving is dangerous; one-sided garlic kissing challenges the other's senses; and funeral laughs offend the bereaved.

What is it about the permissible elements in blackmail that make blackmail morally impermissible? One answer is that failure to comply to the blackmailer's request means that the blackmailed are harmed by unwanted exposure. Further, compliance with the request means that they are harmed by financial loss. There are, though, numerous – all seemingly morally permissible – instances of combinations with such features. 'If you keep on drinking, I'll divorce you.' 'If we

don't get bonus payments, we'll resign and work abroad.'
'If taxes increase, we'll incorporate our business offshore.'
True, the latter two examples in recent years have received
public distaste with regard to bankers, but the ethos of capi-
talist society is to encourage efficient economic competition,
including minimizing tax liabilities where legal.

To sort out the blackmail puzzle, we must resist accepting
so readily that the components of blackmail are individually
morally permissible. Let us take two extreme cases, relating
them to Dan, our blackmailed man.

Here is one extreme. Dan has been involved in some shady
arms dealings that merit public exposure. Such exposure
would focus the authorities on legal loopholes that need clos-
ing. Perhaps Dan's activities have, indeed, been criminal. In
such cases, blackmail is wrong because the blackmailer is
offering to connive with Dan in a cover-up. The blackmailer
ought to be exposing the activities rather than trying to benefit financially by keeping them under wraps. Dan may pay to
preserve the cover-up of his activities; but, whether he does
so or not, he deserves to be exposed.

Here is a case at the other extreme. Dan has not been
engaged in anything that merits public interest. He has been
indulging in some private sexual peccadilloes that would
embarrass him, if made public – but peccadilloes that harm
no one. In this case, the blackmailer is trying to make money
out of doing something that is wrong – namely, the public
humiliation of Dan. Dan may, of course, pay up to avoid the

embarrassment; but, whether he does so or not, he does not deserve exposure.

In these two cases the blackmailer is intent on doing something wrong, either by way of covering up what ought to be uncovered or by threatening to expose what merits no exposure. And that is what is wrong with blackmail in less extreme cases – ones, though, that may be difficult to assess regarding the right thing to do. For example, third parties may discover that some church members use prostitutes and that political leaders who condemn the use of drugs indulge themselves. Sometimes it may be right to expose such matters; sometimes not. The motivation to expose, or not, should not depend on the exposers' potential financial benefit. The motivation should be that of doing the right thing.

*   *   *

Casting couches have, so the tales go, been scenes of wrong motivations. Film directors should cast actresses according to their suitability for roles to be played, not their suitability as sexual partners for directors (unless, arguably, auditioning for that sort of film). Appointment boards should appoint according to candidates' job suitability, not their 'old school tie'.

What of the cases cited earlier that appear similar to blackmail – the investment managers who threaten to resign without bonuses; the directors, to leave the country; and the wife, to argue for divorce? Grey areas arise: sometimes we treat them as blackmail; sometimes as permissible. Certain investment managers may contribute hugely to a nation's wealth; directors are meant to run companies tax-efficiently; and people can find married life soul-destroying if spouses are drunkards. Of course, other factors come into play: the managers' demands may be exorbitant – akin to blackmail – and directors are failing to show loyalty. Spouses may be lacking appropriate sympathy during days so dark in marriage.

What is valuable about blackmail, as a puzzle, is that it reminds us that that we should do things for right reasons; and those right reasons do not usually involve threats made purely for selfish monetary gain.

22. THE FROG, THE SCORPION AND 'THOU SHALT NOT'

16. WALK ON BY ... ?

 ### 1. SOMEONE ELSE WILL ...

9

SQUABBLING SAILORS: IF THIS BE DEMOCRACY ...

When seriously ill, you are well advised to visit a doctor, consultant or nurse. If your shoes need to be repaired, sense suggests you should nip to cobblers versed in their trade. To learn the mandolin – well, being taught by mandolin players is best. The call is for experts. No one rational would seek submission to surgeons anatomically ignorant, or want their pianos tuned by those poor at tuning. With regard to how best to solve mathematical, medical and musical problems, we do not urge, 'Let us be democratic'; we do not seek decision by majority votes. Instead, we seek expertise. We do so because we know that majority votes are unreliable means for acquiring what is required where skills and knowledge are concerned. Why, then, turn to the democratic vote to be well governed? As Winston Churchill once quipped, five minutes with average voters should shatter any faith in democracy.

Democracy is pithily summed, in Abraham Lincoln's words, as government of the people, by the people, for the people; but nations possess different criteria for what counts as 'the people' and rule 'of', 'by' and 'for'. Rule 'by the people' means by adults, some informed, many misinformed, voting for representatives or in referendums. Many vote on the basis of self-interest, others on what they perceive best for the country overall. The rule may be by so-called majority votes derived from a rag-bag of differently sized constituencies on a 'first past the post' system or on a proportional basis. Whichever means deployed, there is no good reason to believe that the resultant government and policies will be best or even much good.

Judging what is good for society requires assessments of economics, morality and sociology, involving the causes of crime, alienation and illness, and the socio-economic consequences of taxation levels, nuclear power and going green. No one sincerely believes that the majority of the electorate, or even a significant minority, has much understanding of those matters. True, where experts disagree, the expert majority may be followed; democracy, though, gives the vote, not to experts, but to virtually all; and the 'all' easily swamps those few with relevant expertise.

Why be democratic?

The above anti-democratic considerations derive from Plato's dialogue *The Republic*, written two and a half thousand years ago. Plato reminds us that, when on a ship, we should prefer to be navigated by the expert navigator, not by squabbling sailors – and not by squabbling sailors even if we are the sailors, voting on likely weather conditions and the location of hazards.

Plato's squabbling sailors may be seen as the mob – rule by the mob being an *ochlocracy*, distinguished in the ancient world from democracy. 'Democracy', in Plato's times, applied to rule by citizens of a certain status: it could be a direct democracy, where relevant citizens would gather in the city's square, argue and then directly vote on proposals. Because of this ancient understanding, James Madison, a founding father of the USA, described the USA as a republic rather than a democracy.

Today's democracies are very different from the ancients'. Today's are usually orientated to professional politicians competing for votes to become representatives of the people. The voting mechanisms are likely to give power to representatives who are persuasive and charismatic, with commercial support. That is one reason why, in some ancient democracies, the leaders would be selected by lottery: it avoids the charismatic charmers having unfair advantage over the plain and bland.

What is wrong with Plato's argument? Plato's ship analogy may be used to attack his position. Plato's navigator is no regular navigator who merely sails his passengers to their chosen destination. Plato's navigator sees his professional duties as extending to choice of routes and destination. It is as if a waiter's role is not merely to take your order and serve dinner, but also to tell you what you must eat. Mind you, this happens in some restaurants.

The above criticism of Plato's analogy has its own defects. It suggests that there are significant areas of political decision-making that should be determined simply by what people happen to want. At the restaurant, I may fancy lamb today rather than salmon. Society, though, is far from that simple. Even in the restaurant, there could be discussion about which is better for me, given my heart condition or concern for animal welfare. Citizens may mistakenly think, for example, that their best interests and society's are served by tax reduction for those already relatively well-off.

The criticism of Plato's analogy may also give rise to the crude and mistaken idea that, with regard to values, one person's opinion and hence vote is as good as another's – as if 'anything goes' with regard to what is right and what is wrong. Plato reminds us, albeit with exaggeration, that we can make mistakes about routes and destinations – about what is worthy of desire and which values a society should prize. This may point to the ideal, very much an ideal, of a very small direct democracy in which well-informed people debate and discuss, reaching an unanimous view about the best way to run their society. There is, though, no reason to think that, even with maximum good will – with all voters intelligently seeking the best for society – there would be agreement about the best means and ends. Reflection and a moral sense, for example, lead well-meaning people to value fair treatment; but disagreements still arise over what counts as fairness in, say, taxation, university admissions, and welfare benefits.

*　　　*　　　*

Priorities conflict. Democratic voting is machinery for delivering decisions; and, whatever the decisions, voters have at least participated in the mechanism. That may increase the likelihood of consent to the resultant government and laws. You as voter take part; but, of course, if the electoral mechanism delivers a result opposed to your vote – if you are in a minority – then you may be alienated by the result, with your liberty infringed. You may have voted for voluntary euthanasia, legalized brothels and high levels of inheritance tax, yet the elected government legislates in a different direction. You cannot then identify with that society's values.

People are part of the electoral process, even when their voting choices are severely limited and ineffectual. That is the advantage of an illusion – but politicians do, at least, have to battle for votes, so they seek to appeal to many of those likely to vote. The appeal, though, is typically in terms of voters' perceived short-term interests.

More fundamentally, perhaps democracy is valuable because it promotes equality and liberty. With the exception of children, the insane and certain other groups, everyone has a right to vote. Hence the voters, it is said, are governing themselves: they are autonomous agents rather than recipients of diktats. That is, though, highly misleading – for, as mentioned, those voters in the minority may well suffer laws opposed to their preferences.

Maybe democracy is valuable because it emphasizes respect for people's rights, not so much because of the right to vote, but because of the vetoes which respect for people demands. Vetoes protect individuals from tyrannies, be they of the majority, of custom, of a powerful state – or, indeed, of minorities seeking to take control.

Plato's ship metaphor leads us well: democracies need navigators to navigate us away from tyrannies, whatever the votes may be. The perennial problem is that we do, of course, have conflicting and muddled aims. At least democracies allow the muddle to be voiced. It is that muddled voice which gives us variety and criticism. And so, as recommended by E. M. Forster many decades ago, despite its illusions, inefficiencies and dangers, democracy arguably does merit the 'two cheers'.

26. PREFERENCES: AVOIDING THE MONEY PUMP

16. WALK ON BY ... ?

28. ON HOW GOOD PUNISHMENT IS BAD, SO BAD

10

MISFORTUNE, MISS FORTUNA – AND MALICIOUS DELIGHT

'Happy is the man whose best friend falls off a roof,' said Confucius. That comment is at the heart of the puzzle. To give it meat, conjure up a fictional figure.

> Lady Assured was until yesterday a high-ranking government minister. Civil servants agreed that she did her job exceptionally well, though she was somewhat arrogant. Today her world crashed. She had been overheard, in private conversation, making some tactless remarks about the Prime Minister; she also spoke of her support for fox-hunting, despite having voted against it; and, on top of that, her department had managed to lose confidential data. Today's newspaper headlines scream against Lady Assured. She resigns.

How should we react to such news? Of course, we may have no view; but some people would feel sorry for her.

People often make tactless remarks privately with the remarks remaining private. Government ministers have to toe party lines, for example concerning fox-hunting, even if the lines conflict with personal beliefs. Further, Lady Assured was unlucky with the data loss: misfortune struck. Lady Assured did the decent thing, taking responsibility: 'the buck stops here'.

The puzzle here, though, concerns *schadenfreude*. That is, it concerns those people who take some pleasure in Lady Assured's misfortune. They cannot help but smile. Many of us, at certain times, experience *schadenfreude* – despite quips about how only the Germans have a special word for the feeling. In Britain at the 1997 election, millions took pleasure in seeing the then young and conceited government minister Michael Portillo lose.

Schadenfreude, though, is understood as malicious. The odds are already stacked against it, if we are wondering whether it is wrong. People usually feel it unworthy of a good person; but why? May there not be something good about the existence of *schadenfreude*?

Can *schadenfreude* be a good thing?

Suppose you take delight in someone else suffering, in cases such as a burglar having been caught and beaten, or a drunk driver fined. Your delight may be because the individuals deserved what they suffered. That it is a matter of desert may indicate that the delight is not malicious. Some people may be pleased about Lady Assured's downfall simply because they judge hypocrisy merits a fall from grace.

Some high-minded individuals would argue that any delight through people's suffering can only be justified if the suffering is a necessary albeit unfortunate result of justice being done. The delight should be in the maintenance of justice rather than in the suffering. Indeed, we can – perhaps we should – pity the person who justly suffers. 'It hurts me more than it hurts you' is the quip of old-fashioned headmasters caning bright pupils. They may feel sorry for the boys caught stealing apples, yet pleased that they were caught and are taking their punishment.

Even when desert is not at issue, we sometimes experience feelings of delight about a misfortune – feelings justified on consequential grounds. Supporters of fox-hunting may be pleased about Lady Assured's downfall because the downfall could lead to the anti-hunting law being repealed. They may also feel sorry for Lady Assured having to suffer. They may argue that their delight is in the likely consequences rather than in the Lady's misfortune.

Desert and consequences for particular projects drift us away from *schadenfreude* pure and unsullied. The pleasures of revenge also drift us away – for the subjects of our *schadenfreude* may have done us no harm. Sometimes we may simply experience pleasure in the misfortunes of another. We can experience such pleasure about Lady Assured's fall from grace, but not because we are especially worried about the 'tally ho' or because we believe that ministers ought to have departments in perfect working order. The pleasure in the downfall may be *schadenfreude*, pure and simple. Now, ought that to be condemned as malicious?

Taking pleasure in others' sufferings could suggest that we hope for such sufferings to occur. To hope for others to suffer is surely malicious. Yet it is far from clear that people who experience *schadenfreude* must hope to have the experience. Rather, some misfortunes occur that provide them with the experience. Now, delight in certain types of misfortune clearly manifests a vicious character. People would be amazingly nasty if they delighted in those who were already having a rotten time suffering even more. Consider victims of earthquakes who then undergo yet more harms from aftershocks. Consider the poor whose lives are made worse through war. Nothing can justify taking pleasure in such pains.

If *schadenfreude* is to be justified at all, it needs to be directed at those doing relatively well in the relevant society. Further, it needs, arguably, to be directed to those who are self-satisfied and smug. Perhaps Lady Assured's arrogance stimulated some people's *schadenfreude*. This, though, runs the danger of returning us to desert. The proud deserve to suffer a fall; the arrogant deserve to be humbled. Once again, we meet the high-minded stance. The stance is that the pleasure ought to be in people getting what they deserve, not in the suffering.

If so, then justifying *schadenfreude* directly, without reference to desert, has once again failed.

*   *   *

Let us see if justified *schadenfreude* can be prevented from collapsing into pleasure at people getting what they deserve.

You watch a confident man in a fine suit, walking out, swivelling his cane – but a moment later, he is victim of a well-aiming pigeon or heavy storm. That can cause us delight, not merely at the incongruity, with the resultant laughter. The man does not deserve the little mishap. The pigeon and storm were unexpected and outside his control: he was suddenly at their mercy. He was unlucky. Lady Assured hit unlucky about the loss of confidential data. Her downfall, the object of our *schadenfreude*, could have resulted solely from that misfortune. What do such examples show?

The man and Lady Assured are shown to be equal to us all in being exposed to Miss Fortuna, being at the mercy of misfortune, of chance. Machiavelli spoke of Fortuna as a woman whom we may try to discipline, yet to whom, in the end, we are all vulnerable.

The man's fine suit, the silver-topped cane, the confident gaze, parade someone safe, utterly safe from life's vicissitudes; yet the pigeon's digestion, the storm, prove otherwise. Lady Assured's high position suggested security; yet, through bad luck, the security crumbled. These misfortunes highlight our common frailty. They restore the equality of human beings in the face of Miss Fortuna. *Schadenfreude* celebrates the restoration.

Is *schadenfreude*'s celebration thereby malicious and unworthy? Some would claim that such examples merely show that we are envious of others' success. No doubt that is sometimes true, but not always. Indeed, if things are going too well for us, we may delight in a touch of *schadenfreude* about ourselves – when we fall. *Schadenfreude* relies on a sense of humanity, of how we all sail on life's oceans of uncertainty.

Harold Macmillan, a former British Prime Minister, when asked about what determined his policies, spoke of, 'Events, dear boy, events.' *Schadenfreude* is delight in recognizing that 'Events, dear boy, events', otherwise known as Miss Fortuna – be she in the form of lost data, an unexpected storm or a careless pigeon – bind us all.

 6. MODESTY AND SHAME: A CAT AND MOUSE TALE

 8. GOING FOR COVER – FROM ARMS DEALING TO CASTING COUCHES

12. WHAT SORT OF CHILDREN SHOULD THERE BE?

11

A GOAT WITH GAPS

I have a goat – one goat only. She sits quietly and still on my left, listening to Purcell. In front of me is a doorway. Through the doorway wanders a creature – a goat. She looks like mine. I can still spy my goat to the left; so the doorway goat is no goat of mine. What I saw afforded me no evidence that the entering beast is my goat; mine still sits, quietly and still, on my left. One goat cannot wholly be in two spatially distinct and discontinuous places at the same time. One goat cannot be two.

I have a goat – as before. She sits, quietly and still, on my left, listening to Purcell. I nod off. When I wake, a few minutes later, no animal is there to my left. A creature wanders through the doorway – a goat. She looks like mine. What I see affords me *some* evidence for thinking the doorway creature is my goatish beast. With no other goat in the

vicinity – I check – I conclude that the goat wandering in is indeed mine. One goat can change its location over a period of time.

One goat can change its location over a period of time; but must there not be spatial continuity and proximity between its locations over that time? Must it not be possible to trace a spatially continuous line, through time, of the goat's locations from, in this example, its position on my left and its later position in the doorway? Such spatial continuity is, of course, expected; but *must* such spatial continuity exist for my goat to be one and the same goat over time? Puzzlingly, many people think so.

Must my goat exist without gaps over time?

Suppose the nodding-off scenario as before, yet with absolutely no sign of my goat having tiptoed round my sleeping form; no sign of my goat having skipped through an open window, then having raced round to the doorway; no sign of the house having been de-roofed, a crane having lifted my goat, the goat then being dropped unharmed and unfazed at the doorway (the roof being neatly returned to the correct position). To sum up, there is no sign at all of continuous movement by the aforementioned goat from my left to the doorway. Yet various signs – love of Purcell, birthmark near left hoof (front), familiar dulcet tones – all point to the beast that now enters being my goat. Why should we insist that, for her to be my goat, the selfsame goat, she must have travelled across continuous spatial locations from my left to the doorway?

Some insist for the following reason. Suppose the discontinuity were to occur: perhaps for some time my goat ceases to exist, then seemingly re-appears in a new location without passing through adjacent locations. Assuming such discontinuities are accepted, we could then conceive of different circumstances after my goat vanishes: for example, two goats subsequently appear, one to my left, one to my right. They both look just like mine. Without spatial continuity there would be no good reason for my believing my goat to have re-appeared on the left rather than on the right.

And my single goat could not now somehow manage to exist in two places at once.

Because of the above replication possibility – and we could expand the story from two to any number of goats, and to vast distances between them – the single goat now appearing in the doorway, after a discontinuity, cannot be mine. A single case of discontinuity brings about a conceivable case of multi-goats – and with a twosome or more, there would be nothing that made one of the resultant goats my original goat.

Can we, though, uncover a feature that, outweighing the lack of spatial continuity, preserves the identity of the goat as my goat?

We return to my goat. I know her well. I take her for walks; I listen to Purcell with her. She is pretty and a pretty constant companion. To date, she is a regular goat. One day an odd thing happens. As she frolics in the field, she vanishes before my very eyes. Her disappearance is for but a few minutes. Perhaps I was distracted; perhaps I have imbibed excess whisky and am tired. Thereafter, every few days, similar gaps in her life – goaty gaps – occur; perhaps they even become prolonged. Others notice the gapping. Here, we could develop different stories. After each disappearance, she reappears in exactly the same location and state as before, or maybe she is a few minutes' distance further on, at average goat travelling speed. Her goat's goatee is in the exact position relative to her body as a few minutes earlier – or maybe it is now more ruffled, in line with the blowing of the wind.

Scientists investigate. They are baffled. Their tests show that in all respects, despite the gaps, she is qualitatively the same goat. Two £1 coins, though, are qualitatively the same; yet one is mine, the other is yours. The coins are numerically different. So, is the goat that appears *my* – numerically the same – goat each time?

There could be motives for different answers. On the one hand, maybe my goat has just won the annual goatish prize, with a lucrative contract. So, this goat appearing after a few minutes' delay, or this goat coming through the doorway, had better still be mine. On the other hand, maybe I have an insurance policy that pays out on my goat's demise; so I would prefer this goat before me not to be deemed mine. But whether this goat is my goat is surely not an arbitrary decision or deeming. There must be some facts of the matter.

What facts can there be, once we have run through shape, hoof-prints and bleat patterns, through genes and iris scans? The answer, given earlier, is: spatial continuity. But why should that be thought a necessary condition for numerical sameness? In learning the term 'same' in the sense of 'one and the same individual', spatial continuity is typically present – but that does not show that it is essential to our grasp of 'one and the same'.

My gappy goat, frolicking in the field, retains a regularity in activity and structure, despite the gaps. When I feed her, even if some goatish gaps then occur, she remains fed (for a bit); if she becomes 'with kid', her pregnancy continues roughly for the typical duration – and so on. To deploy a suggestion from the great seventeenth-century Leibniz, for there to be the same continuing individual, there must be an active principle of unity. Unity through regularity is the key. In our regular world, this regularity underlies the usual gap-free continuity; but, as our goat tale shows, such underlying regularity is consistent with spatial gaps. My goat remains a unity, albeit with gaps.

When regularity has gone, we doubt sameness of item. When the bottle is smashed, destroyed, the smithereens do not perform as one. After the mother gives birth, the behaviour of the child soon lacks spatial regularity in relationship to mother. It is the regularity in behaviour that holds an item – a creature – together as a unity. Such regularity leads us to think of a swarm of bees, even a flock of sheep, as items with some unity.

*   *   *

The proposed 'active principle of unity' for an item to remain the same, even a gappy one, may itself appear exposed to replication puzzles. After a gap, two or two hundred and two goats could appear, all exhibiting the same regularity with the original. We should be unable to determine which one is my goat.

The replication argument, though, could also be used against the sameness of any standard spatio-temporally continuous entity, such as a goat. We could dream up thought-experiments whereby a regular goat spontaneously divides into numerous goats all like the original. We could therefore argue that even with a single goat, the existence of a goat a moment later cannot be taken to be the existence of the same goat. Yet that conclusion would be absurd – for we should have lost all idea of one and the same entity persisting through time.

Of course, gaps could get out of hand. We could imagine goats ceasing to be, then popping up years later in different parts of the universe. We may then anguish philosophically whether they could be numerically the same goats. In such cases, the required principle of unity would seem to be lacking – though who knows quite what is being imagined in such bizarre cases?

Thought-experiments need to be handled with care. Our concepts are grounded in this world to date. If possible replications are to be treated seriously, they cannot be used to undermine our normal understanding of items remaining numerically the same through time. Our modest gappy goat tale is a thought-experiment, but it is not one thought too far. It makes perfectly good sense. My goat may continue as my goat, numerically the same, even with the gaps.

Thus we see how what makes a creature one and the same creature over time is neither spatial continuity nor arbitrary linguistic decision. Rather, it is a question of how well the creature, the biological chunk, hangs together. Pondering further, we should see that that applies as much to human beings as to goats. For your human life to be the selfsame life through time – well, how well do your values, memories and intentions, your character traits, physical features and abilities, hang together?

18. TIME FOR ZOOLOGICAL INVESTIGATIONS – FROM THE BEDROOM

25. PIN DROPPING

21. SPEAKING OF WHOM?

 1. SOMEONE ELSE WILL ...

12

WHAT SORT OF CHILDREN
SHOULD THERE BE?

People typically desire the best for their children; and, when they have that desire, the children are usually already existing – but only usually. We sometimes wonder about the best for children, prior to their existence. These days, concerned would-be parents, even before conceiving, may eat appropriately, resist smoking and alcohol, and undergo medical tests to check all will be well. Concern for healthy offspring means that women, once pregnant, are advised over a whole range of factors – from scans to vitamins to, for all I know, eye-liner choice.

Now, there are some tragic cases – painful dilemmas – when a foetus is so badly deformed that most doctors would recommend abortion: 'better to try again later'. There are also more controversial cases, also tragic, when some would recommend abortion, others not, depending upon likely disablement. Let us, though, avoid the emotional turmoil of possible abortions. Let us, at this stage at least, solely consider pre-conception cases.

A woman is wanting a child, but she has a serious medical problem, a chemical imbalance, such that were she to conceive now, the child born would be disabled. Doctors point out that if she delays conception for a few months, by which time her health would be fine, then all would go well for the forthcoming child.

> 'It would be better for your child and for you, if you delay conception.'

That paradoxical claim is, well, paradoxical. How can it be better for the child? If the delay happens, then the child who would otherwise have been born fails to be born. Someone else would be born, because the particular egg and spermatozoon would then be different from those now. A question that raises the perplexities here is:

Can there be a wrongful birth?

Most people, in the circumstances cited, would delay conception. Surely, that is the right thing to do. If that is the right thing to do, then there must be something wrong about the choice of a woman who goes ahead now with the conception. Yet suppose that she does just that – and the resultant child, disabled, grows up. What harm, if any, has been done?

Has the child been harmed? Had the conception not occurred, the child would not have existed; so the harm, if at all, must hang on whether the child's life is, in some way, a harm overall for him, through too much suffering, inability to look after himself when grown up – or whatever. There are two cases: one in which he is overall harmed; and one in which he is not.

If he suffers so much that he sincerely and consistently believes he would rather not have been born, then he has been harmed: he has been harmed by being brought into existence. So, if such suffering and resultant attitude is pretty likely to occur, that is a good reason for delaying conception rather than conceiving such a child now. However severely disabled he is, though, he may genuinely value being alive, and so no net harm has been done to him by conceiving him. Had conception been delayed, he would have lost that valuable life.

The considerations above all hang on the likelihood of the child valuing his life; but that is far from the whole story. Remember, we have been considering the position before the child is even conceived. If – and this is a big 'if' – we can make sense of the interests of people even before they are conceived, then we should take into account the interests of others who could have been conceived, but because the woman went ahead with the conception now, they were not conceived.

Once we reflect on how different children could have been created, had conceptions been delayed, be they delayed by hours, days or months, we should recognize that we are inevitably choosing between different possible individuals. If the woman delays conception, the disabled child is not created, but a healthy child is created later on. If the woman does not delay, then the disabled child is created, but not the healthy one. Whatever the choices, many possible children are being selected against. Although many people find it obnoxious to be choosing between children, this in a way is what happens.

Selection between would-be children may be made, of course, not with the interests of the different possible children at heart, but with other interests, such as economic factors. Such factors account for the preference in some societies to have boys rather than girls. Sometimes parents may deliberately conceive an additional child – a 'saviour child' – in order to provide matching bone marrow to help save an existing child. The creation of children can result from a mishmash of motives – and often, of course, the motive of child creation is completely absent, yet sexual intoxication very much present.

Given choices have to be made, it is better to choose the outcome which is likely to be the happiest child. Naturally, this is where disputes can arise. Many of us would be appalled at deaf parents deliberately preferring their child to be deaf rather than permitting medical interventions, be it on themselves or the embryo or the baby, to prevent or cure the deafness. Yet such parents might argue that their family life would be better with the child deaf — and better for the child. We should, though, resist their argument for it appears to justify such deaf parents deliberately causing deafness in their offspring, if born with good hearing.

Perhaps the picture of choosing between possible children is misleading — as if there are numerous possible children, lingering in shadowy waiting rooms, awaiting conception. Choosing between them seems personal: we are discriminating against one in favour of another. Now, of course, we frequently do choose between people — we may prefer the raven-haired to the blonde — even though in many walks of life such discrimination is condemned. With regard to the conception question, though, we are not directly discriminating between individuals — they do not yet exist — but assessing which features anyone would prefer to have, if existing. We cannot harm or benefit someone who does not exist. Harms and benefits need existent individuals.

*   *   *

Assessing which features anyone would prefer to possess does not imply disrespect for existent people who lack the preferred features. To note that anyone, for example, would prefer not to be paralysed does not remotely imply that we lack respect for people who are paralysed. Consider an analogy: valuing contraceptive use does not suggest a disrespect for existent people.

In choosing when to conceive, to avoid creation of individuals with unfortunate features, we inevitably are led into considering which treatments and enhancements we should, or should not, be prepared to permit for foetuses, embryos or women yet to conceive. After all, for existing children, we accept vaccinations – and we correct speech impediments, irregular teeth, even flat feet. Many parents, financially fortunate, arrange additional tuition for their children in the hope of intellectual, linguistic, mathematical improvements.

Now, suppose foetuses or mothers prior to conception could be 'treated' to enhance the future children's intelligence, moral awareness, even feelings of well-being. What objections could there be to such treatment?

Somewhere along the line we feel uneasy at interferences to make individuals better; maybe we are uneasy at the underlying promotion of competitiveness. Usually, though, we are keen to make existing people better; so, in addition, why not, from the very start, make better people?

32. LIFE WITHOUT END: TOO MUCH OF A GOOD THING?

 1. SOMEONE ELSE WILL ...

17. LET THE MUSIC PLAY

13

THE CARD-SHARP CAMEL *or* '**YOUR NUMBER'S UP**'

Encountering a camel, when in the desert, is to be expected, but finding a humped card-sharp, sitting at a table outside a Soho club, wearing shades, smoking a cigar – well, we are, to say the least, a little surprised.

'Here's a little game suited for you two, suited because I can see that you are perfectly rational individuals, able to work things out – unusual for round here,' smirks the Camel. With that she deals us two cards face down, one for my friend Ariadne, one for me, telling us that they are cards from a pack of one hundred, numbered from 1 to 100.

I look at my card, Ariadne at hers; but we cannot see the other's card.

Camel adds, with a glint in her eye, the glint sneaking out from behind puffs of cigar smoke, that we cannot tell just by reasoning, reasoning separately from each other, who has the

JUST THINK RATIONALLY—
IGNORING THE FACT THAT I'M
A CAMEL, OF COURSE...

lower number. Well, with the flattery of rationality seducing us, we each quietly reflect, to see what we can conclude from Camel's comments, I from the card before my very eyes, and Ariadne from hers. Camel is insistent that we should do our very best by way of reason, but quietly and separately.

A moment's muse tells me that Ariadne clearly has not found herself with card number 1 – after all, she would then know straight away that she has the lower card. Camel would not have dealt her number 1 – and indeed I do not have card number 1.

To make the set-up vivid, I own up to readers, but not to Ariadne, that I find myself with 29. Maybe Ariadne has 63, though, to repeat, I am ignorant of which card she has been dealt. Clearly, in such a case – and there are many more – both Ariadne and I would readily agree that we are unable to figure out who has the lower.

I can see my number, number 29. Moving on from my reasoning that Ariadne cannot have number 1, I reason that Ariadne will also have reasoned that I cannot have number 1, otherwise I would know that I have the lower.

So (it seems) we must both know that number 1 is ruled out. Now, if Ariadne has card number 2, then that must be the lower number. We both know, though, courtesy of Camel, that we cannot tell who has the lower, so obviously Ariadne lacks number 2; and she will have ruled out my having 2.

And so the reasoning continues, with each of us (separately, silently) ruling out 3 next and then 4 and so forth. By such reasoning, we should rule out our having any numbered cards at all. Yet that cannot be right: we have two distinct cards, one of which is the lower numbered. That the reasoning goes wrong will be before my very eyes, when it reaches as far as ruling out 29. Yet, how does the reasoning go wrong? No wonder Camel smiles smugly – well, for a Camel.

What goes wrong with the reasoning?

We have Camel's clear statement, which we summarize as:

C: Neither of you can work out who has the lower card.

We each have that statement to consider, against the background of our being rational, seeing one card each, keeping quiet, no peeking and so forth.

Suppose I were to have card number 1, then I would rightly judge that C is false. The evidence of my eyes easily outweighs what I heard from Camel – not because I have better eyesight than hearing, but because there are better explanations for what I heard being wrong than for what I see being an illusion. Now, I do not have card number 1, but how do I know that Ariadne lacks that card?

Were Ariadne to have number 1, then that would show to Ariadne, but not to me, that C is false. So, before the paradoxical reasoning can move up the numbers, we both need to recognize that neither of us has number 1.

The mutual recognition that neither of us has 1 could be secured by our publicly announcing it or by Camel, flicking through the remaining cards, displaying card number 1. Were 1 to be ruled out in such a way, we should then possess common knowledge: that is, not merely would we mutually know that neither has number 1, but I would also know that Ariadne knows that I know that she knows – and so forth – that we both lack card number 1.

Possessing such common knowledge, our reasoning would move to: 'What if one of us has card number 2?' As with card number 1 being ruled out, so card number 2 could be ruled out by public announcements or Camel's display of that card, drawing it from the pack's remaining cards.

And so on …

If cards, one by one, are gradually ruled out in public, with Ariadne and I recognizing this, then Camel will look more and more irritable through her puffs of smoke, for, at some stage, the 'and so on' of the paradoxical reasoning will be blocked. Ariadne or I will be unable to confirm lack of the relevant card. One of us will have it – and will know it to be the lower because all lower numbered cards will have been eliminated. At that stage, Camel's C claim would be shown to be false. This, though, only comes about because of the public displays whereby we both know that the other lower cards are ruled out as held by us.

Arguably, the above discussion shows that common knowledge is required for the paradoxical reasoning to be justified in ruling out the cards. So, the paradoxical reasoning goes wrong because it illegitimately assumes such knowledge – when such knowledge is absent. If nothing is said by either of us, we have the possibility that the other has card 1 and that Camel has misled us in saying that neither of us can tell who has the lower card.

Suppose, though, that we both truthfully and clearly announce at the beginning, 'Well, I cannot tell who has the lower card.' I now know that Ariadne knows that I know … – and so on – that Camel spoke the truth and that neither of us can work out who has the lower card. That tells us that we, in common, both rule out our having card number 1, but does it show that we both rule out having cards 2, 3, 4, 5?

Neither of us would know how many cards the other would rule out in that way. It is indeterminate. Hence, neither of us can be justified in succumbing to the paradoxical reasoning, ruling out cards one by one, on and on.

*   *   *

'Here,' says Camel, 'We're starting again. See, I've just dealt you a single card, face-down, from a pack numbered 1 to 100. It is the lowest card that I can deal and which you cannot work out which one it is – without looking, of course.'

We wonder at Camel's confidence. We can surely work out some things. Camel would not have dealt us card 1, for that would be the lowest possible card. So, it would not be the lowest card she could deal us, without our knowing it to be the lowest. We guess the lowest must be card number 2 – and we start to utter the word 'two', when we hold back. We realize that we should then know that 2 is the lowest. So, 2 is also ruled out.

We feel queasy. We see how we could run through all the cards. None seems to satisfy the conditions set. If we reason that a particular card is the lowest one, then that fact rules it out, for we would then know – or so it seems.

Camel smiles at the disquiet on our faces. She coolly turns over the card: it is number 1.

'But we did think of that …,' we stumble.

'And so, you ruled it out.' Camel completes our sentence.

We realize the moral. The lowest card Camel could deal was card number 1 – and we knew that. But we used her claim, that we could not know the lowest card, to rule out 1; and hence it was ruled back in – but if we saw that, then we would be ruling it out again. We ought to have stayed our hand, insisting that it was card 1, showing that Camel had been mistaken in saying that we could not work out the lowest card. Well, we would have shown that, unless she had taken our reasoning into account and had dealt us card 2. But then we might have taken all that into account.

And so it is that some things that we can be told disorientate us – for by ruling them out, we must rule them back in and then back out – and so on.

6. MODESTY AND SHAME: A CAT AND MOUSE TALE

23. CREAMY PHILOSOPHERS: WHO KNOWS WHO KNOWS ...

27. A GAZELLE, A SLOTH AND A CHICKEN

14

INDOCTRINATION: WHEN BELIEVING GOES WRONG

Here is a little challenge:

> Try sincerely to believe that Beijing is the capital of Britain, that 2 + 2 makes 5 and that it is right to torture children for the sheer fun of it. Try sincerely to believe that promethium has atomic number 61.

For the sake of this chapter, let us hope that you cannot believe the first three suggestions. And, unless you already have knowledge of the periodic table – or believe this book to be an authority on such matters – let us hope you cannot just believe the final suggestion. The point is that people cannot simply switch on a belief; people cannot believe at will. Beliefs are switched on by the world, often by years of schooling. Let us consider outlines of three school teachings, deliberately presented in a stark, extreme manner – to afford focus.

A certain Fundamentalist School teaches that the Bible holds the truth regarding the world's creation, how we ought to live, and how God judges behaviour and offers eternal life. If pupils question these claims, the teachers point them to some historical evidence for the Bible's accuracy, the authority of the Church – and the need for faith.

A Science School teaches evolutionary theory and that religious texts are not to be relied upon for scientific fact. If pupils question, the teachers point them to some fossil and genetic evidence, some extracts from Darwin and mention the authority of eminent working scientists. The ultimate authority is scientific investigation.

A Nazi School, at one stage, forced Jewish pupils to sit separately from German pupils. If pupils questioned, they were told that Germans had superior blood running in their veins. The pupils were taught of Germany's glory and its destiny for expansion, taking over Poland and Russia. The Führer knew best.

Most people consider the Nazi School as indoctrinating. Some people view the Fundamentalist School as engaged in some degree of indoctrination. These schools contrast with the Science School. Yet some would claim that the fundamentalist teaching is no more indoctrination than the science teaching. All schools rely on approved text books; they have teachers with certain views, sometimes with an official state line to promote. Pupils typically lap up what they are taught – as many did in Nazi Germany.

As adults, we are not immune to our beliefs being manipulated – 'coaxed' – by various authorities. When women pay exorbitant sums for wonder creams, convinced of rejuvenating powers, executives rub hands with glee at their advertising success. If politicians receive increasing support because of stories placed in the press, they trumpet (well, to themselves) their persuasive skills.

In addition to the above ways of coming to believe – ways that may have a feel of indoctrination – there are the blatant examples of indoctrination, of brainwashing, where victims are broken down psychologically. The victims find themselves simply accepting and believing, it seems, whatever they are told. Such examples are reported by certain survivors of North Korean and Soviet prisons, and others.

How, then, should we learn about the world?

How does education differ from indoctrination?

The difference lies not in the content. We may be indoctrinated with the truth; and education is likely to include some mistaken beliefs. The difference lies not in the perpetrators' intentions, for both indoctrinators and educators may intend the best for recipients, by way of access to perceived truth, flourishing lives and even afterlives.

Indoctrination 'proper', it has been argued, involves force. The recipients' psychological states have been caused by certain external factors, drugs and torture. In the school context of weak indoctrination, the causes may be charismatic teachers, restricted reading and repeated mantras.

Resting indoctrination's distinctiveness on the beliefs *being caused* deserves challenge. Most beliefs have, in a way, been forced upon us – by experiences. Turning your head, you see the train approaching, and, as a result, believe that it is indeed approaching and you had better move quickly. The belief has been caused by what you saw. Someone might even have forced you to look, to warn you. Causes, even blatant force, can be benign, giving us true beliefs – causes can also be the opposite. Consider the following.

I tell my friends that Prince Charles has relinquished his right to the throne and is living in a tent. Friends look baffled – then they twig. 'Ah, you fell for that April Fools' report. Mind you, you were drunk.' I should then be irrational in clinging to my belief, now learning of its causal source.

Whether I should stick with my beliefs depends on the evidence, and that includes taking into account how they arise. We may now relate that thought to the difference between indoctrination and education.

The psychological states – how they feel 'from within', the phenomenology – may be the same, whether resulting from indoctrination or not, whether they have been blatantly forced by drugs or simply the Bible or *Scientific American* readings – or by directly experiencing the world. Further, the indoctrinated and regular believers may appear the same 'from without': that is, they behave similarly. There is, though, one big difference in potential behaviour; namely, their responses to evidence that runs counter to their beliefs.

Indoctrination provides a protective belt, a belt that shields believers from counter-evidence. Education encourages an openness to evidence. Whether the indoctrination be political, commercial or religious – be it glorification of the state, Western belief in free enterprise and that no child should be without a PlayStation, or the Qur'an interpreted as justifying stoning – the outcome is a block on questioning, criticism and further investigations.

The indoctrinated yield to no challenge to their belief: any challenge is reinterpreted, explained away or simply ignored. Indeed, we may value this stance to a limited extent in certain areas: witness how blind – and delicious – love can be. Yet, to get around the world – to flourish in the world – we have to be responsive to the world, to the evidence and to changes. Full-blown indoctrination is designed to prevent such responsiveness. Education is designed to embrace it. That is why education is preferable to indoctrination.

*　　　*　　　*

Indoctrination comes in degrees. Religious believers often allow room for criticism, but within certain boundaries. On some subjects the Pope's word, for example, is treated as infallible. A newspaper gives space to opposing opinions, yet ensures that its news presentation is appropriately politically slanted.

When indoctrination is at the extreme, we may wonder whether indoctrinated 'beliefs' are beliefs at all. If you properly believe something, you believe it is true – even though it may, of course, be false. Because of the truth-aim, beliefs to be beliefs need to be responsive, sensitive, to evidence. Being open to evidence, to hearing opposing views, does not mean, though, that all views deserve equal respect.

All views certainly do not deserve equal respect. Some are just false; some are morally horrendous. Yet, in line with John Stuart Mill's liberalism, it is arguably better to have them aired than silenced. They may, after all, stimulate us to find and assert the truth – though, sadly, there is no guarantee.

 **4. RESOLUTIONS, GOOD INTENTIONS –
AND CREAM BUNS**

 **9. SQUABBLING SAILORS: IF THIS
BE DEMOCRACY ...**

**18. TIME FOR ZOOLOGICAL INVESTIGATIONS –
FROM THE BEDROOM**

19. ADDICTED TO LOVE

15

JESTERS, BERTRAND RUSSELL
AND PARADOX

The jesters were not happy. They put their heart into jesting, joking and clowning at the various courts of their employment; but never were they invited to join in and dine at the banquets at which they jested. Rebellion was in the air – their jesting bells jangled – but instead of rebelling, they planned their own banquet, the Jesters' Banquet. More accurately, they would hold a banquet for all and only those jesters ineligible to join in banquets at which they performed their jests. To be eligible for the banquet you must not merely be a jester but also one who jested for people who would not permit you to join in their banquets. All such jesters could join the Jesters' Banquet.

The Jesters' Banquet would be as grand as those of the great courts – dining on swan, with singers and song, even the odd glass of champagne. Arrangements were made, all going according to plan. One day, a thought crossed their jesting minds.

'We must find ourselves a jester to jest for us at our banquet. After all, we don't want to jest ourselves – that would be too much like work.' An excellent idea, they agreed; and, as luck would have it, they happened upon a fresh-faced lad looking for his first jesting job. 'You shall be our Jesting Junior.'

All went well, so well – until today, the banquet day – for here we are, listening in to the singers and song, as the jesters dine and wine at their splendid Jesters' Banquet. They are, of course, somewhat solemn-faced, not wanting themselves to risk working as jesters. Jesting Junior, though, has just performed some fine japes, jokes and jests.

'Come and join the banquet, Junior,' the jesters cry – well, all of them apart from Jesting Stickler, the most stern-faced jester of them all.

'Our banquet is just for jesters ineligible to join in banquets at which they jest,' says Stickler firmly. 'So, Junior, I'm afraid, cannot join us.'

'Oh yes, he can,' answer the others. 'Oh no, he can't,' replies Stickler, with Junior looking suitably baffled.

With the 'can's and 'can't's becoming more ferocious, the argument clearly turning into a fracas, a fight forthcoming, we tiptoe away and reflect on the puzzle.

Is Jesting Junior eligible to join the Banquet?

There is nothing contradictory in jesters being employed to perform at banquets, yet ineligible to indulge and dine.

There is nothing odd about such jesters feeling unloved, even aggrieved, and hence making their own banqueting arrangements as described. Trouble arises with the jesters employing their own jester.

If Jesting Junior is employed by those who do not permit him to dine, then, as the banquet is for all those who work for such stickler employers, he is eligible after all. But if he is eligible to join in the banquet, then, as the banquet is open only to those not allowed to join in the banquets at which they jest, he is surely ineligible.

In summary, the conditions of the banquet mean that Jesting Junior is eligible if and only if he is ineligible. That is contradictory. Typically, logicians would conclude that the banquet cannot exist for it has contradictory membership rules. In humility, we resist such a quick response.

There can exist – no doubt there do exist – institutions, banqueting clubs, corporations, constitutions, with contradictory rules, rules that cannot be consistently applied in all possible circumstances. They may go unnoticed, for circumstances may not arise which exhibit the inconsistencies. Now, if the existence of our Jesters' Banquet hangs on its conditions determining for all *possible* individuals, without contradiction, whether they are eligible to banquet, then indeed the banquet cannot exist. The banquet's conditions fail to give a consistent answer regarding the eligibility of any possible jester. We have brought this to light by actually having a jester, Jesting Junior, jesting for them.

In reality a banquet or institution or club's existence does not hang on its rule book lacking contradictions. We can tell that the Jesters' Banquet exists by the wining and dining. In similar vein, many of us unwittingly hold contradictory beliefs; yet we get through life undefeated by such contradictions. It is even possible (really?) that this book contains the odd contradiction or even quite a few – yet it exists. The Jesters' Banquet exists, but it has a contradictory condition of attendance, if the condition is intended to provide a 'yes or no' answer in all possible circumstances.

*   *   *

Our Jesting Tale is a lead-in to Russell's great paradox which concerns classes or sets. Classes and sets are abstract entities, unlike banquets and jesters.

You are a human being, so you belong to the set of human beings. The set is not itself a human being: it is not made out of flesh and blood; it is not a messy fleshy combination of all humans. It is abstract – as are numbers and the concept of justice. We may meet and eat three apples, but the number three is not something that we can meet and eat.

Whether items are members of the set of humans simply hangs on whether they possess the feature of being human. Pianists, philosophers and princesses are members, but pianos, peacocks and porcupines are not. All members of the set of philosophers are members of the set of humans. The set of philosophers is hence a 'subset' of the set of humans.

Now, the set of philosophers itself is not, of course, a philosopher — a set cannot philosophize — so, it is not a member of itself. The set of pianos is not itself a piano; so it is not a member of itself. Many sets are not members of themselves.

As there are sets that are not members of themselves, there may well be some sets that are members of themselves — and there are. Consider the set of items that are not pork-eaters: it includes some people, lots of other creatures, also turnips, trees and treacle — and also itself. The set of non-pork-eaters is itself a non-pork-eater; so the set of non-pork-eaters includes itself. Were sets containers, then we would doubt that a set could ever be a member of itself — how can a container contain itself? However, sets are not containers.

Time to give Bertrand Russell, Cambridge philosopher and logician of the early twentieth century — also a political activist — a run for his money. By the way, we met him in the Preface.

Russell proposed a set, hereafter the Russell Set. The feature that determines membership of the Russell Set is that members be sets that are not members of themselves. The Russell Set contains the set of readers, the set of berets, the set of cannabis users, for no set is itself a reader, a beret or a cannabis user. The Russell Set does not contain the set of non-pork-eaters, for that set is a member of itself. Now, here comes our jesting and troubling question. Is the Russell Set a member of itself?

Suppose that the Russell Set is a member of itself: then it belongs to the set of items that are not members of themselves; so it is not a member of itself. Suppose that it is not a member of itself: then it qualifies to be a member of the set of items that are not members of themselves; so it is a member of itself. Paradoxically, the Russell Set is a member of itself if and only if it is not a member of itself.

The Russell Set leads us into contradiction, as did the Jesters' Banquet. With the Jesters' Banquet we made sense of how the banquet could exist yet with contradictory conditions for attendance: after all, we could see the banquet in full flow. In contrast, we cannot make sense of the Russell Set existing, albeit with contradictory conditions. We can pick out a set only by the conditions for determining whether items are members or not. Contradictory conditions fix nothing. If given the contradictory instruction, 'Right now, both turn off and don't turn off the light,' there is nothing possible you can do correctly to obey: you are baffled. Similarly, the conditions for the Russell Set fail to determine a set.

Russell's contradiction arises from the feature 'is not a member of itself'. That feature, though, usually gives no trouble. It is intelligible – witness the simple examples given of it above – and it is used to provide perfectly acceptable mathematical results. So, arguably a continuing puzzle is how best to handle the feature – how to justify restricting it – to avoid the paradox.

*   *   *

For Russell, mathematics should possess eternal truth and supreme beauty: 'a beauty cold and austere, like that of sculpture'. Russell's discovery of his paradox was therefore highly unsettling – for the paradox gave but the foothold of shifting sands.

 13. THE CARD-SHARP CAMEL
or **'YOUR NUMBER'S UP'**

29. A KNOWING GOD KNOWS HOW MUCH?

31. INFINITY, INFINITIES AND HILBERT'S HOTEL

16

WALK ON BY ... ?

You know how it is: you saunter along, when you are suddenly aware of a beggar, sitting on the pavement a few yards ahead. Automatically, you quicken your step, trying to ensure that, as you draw near, others will be walking between you and that down-and-out 'other'. Or you cross the road: you really are too busy even to allow your eyes to meet with this other. He may be a charlatan, a con-man, off to wine and dine later that evening; well, there are stories and stories. Or maybe he engages in profitable transactions of a pharmaceutical kind. In any case, you reflect, the state provides. And so, you walk on by. As you walk, you feel some unease.

Or the above may not be so ...

Instead, you feel for change, for small coins – must be neither too little nor too much – quite what is the right amount? Your eyes are averted – true, you are embarrassed – but you slip the coins into those dirty hands. What a relief! At least no

contact – or maybe there was. So, out comes the antiseptic spray; of course out it comes only once you are at a distance suitably discreet. At least you did something; at least you were not touched by a meanness of nature; you feel, indeed, a touch pleased with yourself. And yet, was it enough, or too much? Did you come over as superior? And so, as you walk on, you feel some unease.

∨

Beggars make many of us feel uneasy. Maybe with both scenarios too much sensitivity is on show; but what ought people to do, when so confronted? There would be no dilemma if we lacked the recognition that suffering and extremes of wealth inequality are objectionable. Yet, surely it is up to the state, through social structures and impersonal taxation, to rectify matters. We may even wonder whether the beggars have brought their sorry state upon themselves. Are they victims of bad luck, or have they wittingly made choices that led to their beggarly blight? If they are to blame, why should we care? Let us assume our beggar is genuine and unfortunate.

Is giving to beggars 'for good reasons' intrinsically wrong?

'Charity wounds him who receives.' People who beg, it is claimed often by the well-heeled, are humiliating themselves. The state, if anyone, should provide. If we succumb and give, we are party to the humiliation. Far better not to give. Better still: make begging illegal. But are these things far better?

In true charitable giving, we bestow goods upon recipients, without expectation of reciprocal rewards. It is not simply that beggars *do not* reciprocate. After all, when you make gifts to friends, they may simply say 'thank you'; but the friends *could* reciprocate. Reciprocation, here, does not demand sameness of monetary value, but some similarity of concern and care. Monetary value sometimes has relevance: exceptionally expensive gifts can cause embarrassment, even humiliation, to recipients who could not possibly reciprocate at that level. Well, genuine beggars typically cannot reciprocate at all.

To handle the reciprocation problem, some beggars offer items in return; but that raises the question of their value. If, on the one hand, they are worthless and unwanted, then it is hypocritical to pretend that the donation is really payment for the items: such pretence would manifest failure to respect the beggar. If, on the other hand, the items possess genuine value and are wanted, then we are no longer in the realm of charitable giving. We can buy or resist without qualms. Self-employed salespeople, living on commission, sometimes meet customers who buy simply out of sorrow for the sellers' plight. In such cases, the salespeople may feel humiliated; or, if they have deliberately manipulated the customers' sorrow, then the customers have been humiliated, whether they know it or not.

For painful examples of humiliation, consider the following. A young man – 'Tutankhamen' – stands outside a museum. Totally covered in gold fabric, wearing an Egyptian mask, he is motionless, a bowl on the ground before him. Museum visitors drop money into the bowl. Each time this happens, he comes to life and bows. People – children – pop in further coins, to see him bow again and again. He may remind you of a dog, needing to beg for each morsel. He expresses his gratitude and servility – as a beggar.

With Tutankhamen, maybe the money is for his performance; so, let us look at a purer begging example. On the Paris Metro, a man gets down on his knees – and begs. On his knees, he shuffles along the carriage. The man is expressly humiliating himself, denigrating himself. One human being's relationship to another ought not to be like that. If, though, the man's behaviour is ironic, then the passengers are being humiliated. Witness your own discomfort, if you picture yourself as witness of the man, be he sincere or ironic.

The begging relationship, though, need not be seen as one of humiliation. Get Metro Man up, off his knees. He is then a fellow human being, down on his luck. True, he may be bowed by circumstances, but giver and receiver may recognize their common humanity. Fellow-feeling need not cause humiliation; rather, it engenders sympathy and generosity. Yes, the beggar is helpless. But a cry for help need not be humiliating; and a cry for help is radically better than starvation. As a rabbi has said, 'God stands with the poor person at the door.' Atheists substitute 'Our common humanity' for 'God'.

*   *   *

None of the above promotes begging as therefore desirable. In view of the sheer chance regarding which beggars attract most attention, which ones are genuinely in need, which ones are most deserving, there are good reasons for authorities to aim at greater success in providing for the dispossessed. In view of the way in which many people treat beggars as disgusting and reprehensible – and many beggars are pitiful and abject, sometimes aggressive, sometimes mentally ill – the actuality of much begging is far removed from Metro Man being urged up off his knees into a shining shared humanity. Yet, with all that said, helping others in distress surely takes precedence over the alleged risk of causing humiliation.

Broadening the sources of humiliation, we may feel degraded by our human condition – by suffering the ills of ageing, unable to fend for ourselves, probably one day unable to perform many personal tasks. This is where, like beggars, we turn to others. And this is where, to avoid the risk of charitable help and humiliation, there is talk of human beings possessing a right to ____ – and fill in the gap with basic goods, from food and drink to education to nursing care to other welfare benefits.

Humiliation, of course, is sometimes deliberately imposed upon unwilling victims. Those who suffered horrendously in concentration camps sought to preserve some dignity by dehumanizing their tormenters, viewing them as wild beasts. Suffering as a result of impersonal forces is not, it appears, as bad as from personal deliberation. The tormenters treated their victims *as if* animals or objects; but the victims needed, of course, to be human – for humiliation to occur. Arguably beasts of the field cannot be humiliated, and certainly you cannot humiliate a pebble, tree or robot.

The down-and-outs begging on street corners deserve, of course, to be treated as human beings. That is what they are. That, though, does not mean declining to help for fear of humiliating them. Declining to help can also humiliate. The beggars' humanity should block our temptation to walk on by – or, at least, to walk on by without concern, without serious reflection. The beggar's humanity should also prevent us from seeing things, as we did above, in terms of black and white – of either the beggars being responsible for their plight or not; of them either being sellers with valuable items for offer, or them just pretending to be able to reciprocate. Human beings have a mishmash of characteristics, motives, and fortunes good and bad. That mishmash leads to some people finding themselves begging. That mishmash should make us hesitate before dismissing a beggar. Indeed, that mishmash should stop us from outright dismissal – and arguably in many cases it should lead us to not walk on by.

20. MERCY: TEMPERING AND TAMPERING WITH JUSTICE

10. MISFORTUNE, MISS FORTUNA – AND MALICIOUS DELIGHT

3. THE VIOLINIST: SHOULD YOU UNPLUG?

17

LET THE MUSIC PLAY

When Annie is happy, she may smile and beam; she may walk with a lightness of limb, talk with a lightness of lilt and cook with a hint of the crazed. That is how Annie expresses her happiness, be the happiness a result of having finished a painting, finding an unexpected £50 note or hearing of her grandson's progress. Annie, being a person and neither pebble nor pineapple, is sentient and experiences happiness and sadness, anger and sympathy, fears and hopes. Annie expresses her feelings – her emotions, passions and moods; her loves, lusts and life.

Music too expresses emotions, yet music is not, of course, a sentient being. Music is a sequence of organized sounds, usually composed with much deliberation, though it may also be the roar of the ocean, the sweep of the gales and the song of, er … birdsong. The music itself does not experience pleasure or pain, happiness or sadness, love or fear, yet many of us, the 'music-blind' excepted, readily and paradoxically speak of music expressing such emotions and moods. As the music unfolds, we may hear sadness and yearning within; we may respond to the sounds as sad. What is going on?

To give us undistorted focus, we steer clear of music with words, despite the possible thought that they must be key to music's significance. Words can mingle so closely with the music that we would be unable to spot what, if anything, the music alone expresses. So, listen to an instrumental work that strikes you as particularly expressive. The music may be classic, jazz or pop. The work's title may be suggestive; but focus attention on the sounds. Let me mention a motley few in case they help: Richard Strauss' *Metamorphosen*; Vaughan Williams' *The Lark Ascending*; George Gershwin's *Rhapsody in Blue*; Santana's *Samba Pa Ti*.

We steer away from musical analysis. That certain musical devices and structures give rise to musical phrases expressive of happiness, sadness or other emotions, does not solve the philosophical puzzle of what it is for such phrases to be expressive in those ways.

One immediate response to our puzzle is to deny that music can be expressive. When you express happiness or sadness, hopes or fears, you usually have some objects in mind that are the source of those states. Your mother has now married for money; that is what makes you happy. The movement at your bedside is that of a snake; the snake is what you fear.

Music, though, does not have thoughts; it does not experience objects – so how can it possibly have emotions and feelings to express?

That simple reflection reminds us that music's expression of emotion cannot be understood in the way in which Annie's expression can. That is assuredly true; but instead of concluding that music cannot express emotion, it is wiser to see if we can resolve the puzzle by grasping music's expressiveness differently. Let us remember: it just is true that most people find it appropriate to speak of music as expressing emotions that can move them. It would be paradoxical indeed if we so quickly concluded that they are mistaken – and then went for a drink. That is too easy a way out.

How can music be happy or sad, angry or peaceful?

The same adjectives may be applied to music, also curiously to fictional characters, as to people. 'Happy', 'sad', 'bleak', 'angry' are words we learn to apply to persons, to some other animals, as well as to music. Of course, some may insist that those words have different meanings from the usual, or are metaphorical, when applied to music – but why, then, do such words sound appropriate? Applying 'sad' to a musical phrase is not arbitrary. There exists, it seems, a similarity between the sadness expressed by human gestures and those musical phrases expressive of sadness.

'Similarity' is the key. We need, though, to distinguish similarity from just any connection. We need also to ask: similarity regarding which features? A handkerchief's knot reminds you of the shopping, but the knot neither expresses nor resembles your intended purchases. In contrast, when music causes us to feel sadness – when it arouses feelings of sadness – we may attribute sadness to the music. Music perhaps 'expresses' the emotions which it arouses in us.

The 'arousal' answer is surely mistaken. We may recognize that some music is expressing sadness, yet not experience sadness aroused within us. A sad clown may make us laugh rather than arousing sadness. Looking at things the other way round, a logical puzzle may cause depression, yet not be a depressed puzzle. And when there is a link between the expressive music and the emotion aroused, the 'arousal' explanation goes the wrong way round. It is not because the music arouses sadness that we consider the music sad. It is because the music is sad that it may arouse sadness. By analogy, it would usually be mistaken to claim that your being scared explains why the lion is looking at you hungrily. Rather, it is the lion's salivation and napkin preparations that explain your being scared.

We have been searching for a connection between music and emotion. The arousal theory connects the music to the hearers' emotions – but, as said, hearers can hear music as expressive of sadness without themselves becoming sad.

Some have argued that music's expressiveness results from the composer's emotions when composing; but who knows what composers may be feeling when hurrying to finish their compositions? Composers may write cheerful music without being cheerful.

For music to be happy or sad, angry or solemn, there must be some similarity connections – let us reiterate – with items linked to such emotions. Let us try again to find the connections.

Consider the classic example of the drooping face of a basset hound. It looks sad; it is expressive of sadness. Look into the clouds and you may see menacing faces. Obviously the clouds are not experiencing menace; and the hound may be far from sad. Yet we are not describing them thus on a whim; we are not projecting emotions onto them willy-nilly. The features of the hound's face resemble the features of a person's sadness, when displayed. Similarly – and arguably – sad music is sad because it possesses features that put us in mind of the sadness of people. Obviously, the music does not 'look' sad; but the way in which it moves, its sound contours, may resemble the pace and contours of the movements of sad people. Well, that is the suggestion.

*   *   *

Music is a special case, an intense case, of two features of human life that are mysterious.

First, we use the same words to describe very, very different things. As a result, we often feel that there must be similarities between those things. The words are not ambiguous terms such as 'bank' (river) and 'bank' (financial) or 'entrance' (way in) and 'entrance' (enchant). Yet often the sole similarity appears to be that we use the same words for the items in question. We describe a sound as 'low', yet is it akin to a bridge that is low? With Vaughan Williams' *The Lark Ascending*, we picture a skylark high in the sky; yet what similarity exists between the violin's 'high' notes and the skylark's height and flight?

Secondly, even though well aware that sad music is not itself sad, we may yet experience emotional reactions to the music as to a sad friend. And think how we do this in other areas of life. We can feel sorry for the basset hound solely based on the drooping face, despite knowing how silly that is. We are moved by fictional characters, despite their being fictional. We may be upset by imaginary disasters happening to loved ones, even though we know that they are only imagined and will not happen.

Our human capacity to find similarities and to be moved by appearances is indeed mysterious – or perhaps just the way we are. Our experience of the expressiveness of music is mysterious – or just the way it is.

Some music is deep – but as deep as the oceans are deep? Some music is light – but as light as a feather or the light of day? And some music is sad – but as sad as a person is sad?

Whatever the degree of expressiveness in music, the meaning that we find in music is surely something beyond expression – save by music.

**30. A WHOLE CLOUD OF PHILOSOPHY –
FROM *COGITO ERGO SUM* TO A DROP
OF GRAMMAR**

**33. MINDFUL OF BARBARIANS – WITHIN
AND WITHOUT**

19. ADDICTED TO LOVE

18

TIME FOR ZOOLOGICAL
INVESTIGATIONS – FROM THE BEDROOM

Sophie and Suzie looked out the lodge's window; gloom, misery, despair swamping them. The rain was torrential; cold winds howled. It was the first day of their school field-trip. They were meant to be out and about, from early morning, clad in unseemly Wellington boots, anoraks and hoods, wading through swamps – and for what purpose? To collect evidence to support, or not, a froggy hypothesis, the hypothesis that all frogs are green.

'Who cares about frogs and their colour?' muttered Sophie.

'I bet the teachers already know the answer,' added Suzie.

'It's all pointless – unless the point is to make us suffer,' they groaned in unison, staring at each other despondently.

A bright smile suddenly crossed Sophie's face. 'Look, Suzie, don't you remember our logic lessons the other week?'

Suzie groaned at this memory of another torture. 'Don't mention logic to me – all those 'A's and 'B's and 'if so and so, then such and such' and this following from that – and that from this.'

'Sorry, Suzie, I'll try to avoid the 'A's and 'B's, but this is worth thinking about. Look, suppose all frogs are green.'

'Here we go,' thought Suzie. 'Suppose this; suppose that. But, okay, I'm supposing away.'

'Well, if it really is true that all frogs are green, then it must follow that if we see something that is not green, it cannot be a frog.'

'Even I can grasp that; but so what?'

'I may as well add that if is true that all non-green items are not frogs, then it follows that all frogs are green – so, any frog we meet would have to be green.'

Suzie groaned; but Sophie continued. 'You see, to say that all frogs are green is the same as saying all non-green items are non-frogs.'

'Okay,' yawned Suzie, 'all very interesting; but we'd better get out of bed and get those horrible rubber boots on and face that dreadful rain.'

'You haven't worked it out yet, have you, Suzie? Look, we don't need to leave our beds and this warm lodge at all. There are numerous items around us, right here indoors, that help support the hypothesis that all non-green items are non-frogs – and that means that those items help support the hypothesis that all frogs are green. The two hypotheses amount to the same thing. We can do our zoological researches without getting out of bed.'

And with that, Sophie started writing entries in her research book, listing the evidence she could see in favour of all frogs being green:

One teddy bear (non-frog): pink (non-green);
Two pillows (non-frogs): purple (non-green)
                 – and so forth.

Suzie caught on, and was soon making her own list – 'After all, we don't want to be accused of cheating,' she giggled. Wardrobe/brown. Cat/black. Lampshade/purple. Mouse/grey.

'Mouse?' the girls both squealed – but that's another tale.

How can pink teddy bears be evidence for all frogs being green?

Let us offer a little background: the ground is that of inductive reasoning. Past regularities frequently lead us to expect the regularities to continue into the future. In spotting regularities, we spot similarities in some respects, ignoring various dissimilarities; we also take into account the circumstances of the regularities. Just because all the people we know live in Europe, we ought not to conclude that all people live in Europe. We have been exposed to a biased sample, if we have never reviewed what exists outside Europe.

Inductive reasoning needs handling with care; yet, however great the care, there is no logical guarantee that the regularities noted will continue into the future. Nonetheless, some scientists and logicians – and our common sense – accept that certain past regularities constitute *some* evidence in favour of those regularities continuing. If you encounter many frogs in a variety of environments and each one is green, you have some evidence in favour of the universal generaliza- tion 'All frogs are green'. Those noted froggy instances 'support' the generalization, even though only to some very small degree.

Our paradox – well, Hempel's paradox of confirmation – arises because we assume that instances do support universal generalizations. Consequently, instances of non-green things that are non-frogs – instances such as pink teddy bears, purple pillows and black cats – support the generalization 'All non- green items are non-frogs'. That generalization, though, seems equivalent to 'All frogs are green.' Hence, finding a pink teddy bear appears to point as much to the 'All frogs are green' generalization as finding a green frog. Yet that is highly paradoxical.

What can be done to overcome the paradox – or should we succumb to the conclusion? Well, are we happy with the equivalence between 'All frogs are green' and 'All non-green items are non-frogs', the latter being the 'contrapositive' of the former? When we read those sentences, we focus on different items, frogs with the first, non-green items with the second. Yet, with some reflection, we probably accept that they are saying the same thing about the world. So, what is good evidence for one is, it seems, good evidence for the other.

The paradox, as said, assumes that a generalization is supported to some extent by its instances. That again is highly plausible. How else do we come to accept that these pages can burn, your hands will not turn into copper, and your head will not transform into a yellow balloon tomorrow?

Perhaps we should just accept the paradoxical conclusion. The pink teddy bear, the purple pillows, the black cat, all offer support for the generalization 'All frogs are green'. Or can anything further be said to avoid this conclusion?

*   *   *

Lots more can be said. Here is a little more. Perhaps we have been amiss in casually speaking of support for a generalization, a hypothesis, a claim. Perhaps we should be speaking of the support there may be for our coming to *believe* that the hypothesis is likely to be true. Once in the territory of possible beliefs, we need to attend to pre-existing beliefs and knowledge.

What we already know is that the number of non-green non-froggy items — which include the aforementioned teddy bear, pillows and cat, but also billions of insects and trillions of atoms — vastly exceeds the number of frogs. Further, we accept that frogs form a natural grouping, whereas teddy bears, pillows and cats do not. Further still, in finding certain non-green non-frogs – say, some pink teddy bears – we are as likely to be supporting beliefs such as 'All frogs are yellow', 'All frogs are blue', even 'All frogs are llamas'. Hence, although 'All frogs are green' and 'All non-green items are non-frogs' are equivalent, it does not follow that a pink teddy bear and a green frog provide the same degree of justification for our coming to suspect that all frogs are green.

How should we set about things, when seeking evidence for a proposed universal generalization? Well, in the case at hand, finding some frogs that are green has some value; but, in the right circumstances, finding the pink teddy bear also helps.

Suppose Sophie and Suzie trek out into the swamps, where there are numerous frogs, all ones seen so far green. Sophie then notices something distinctly un-green that is bobbing around: it is pink. It would be useful to establish whether it is a cast-off teddy bear and so no frog. It is worth discovering the item to be a teddy bear – otherwise it could be a pink frog and a counter-example to the froggy hypothesis. Scientific research can involve seeking to refute a proposed hypothesis as much as garnering support.

Paradoxically, instances of a generalization sometimes undermine support for the generalization. Suppose the hypothesis is, 'All green frogs live outside the estates of the Queen'. Well, we encounter lots of frogs outside the estates and indeed they are green. Unless and until more information is available, these frogs would be evidence for green frogs also living within the estates, not their absence. Frogs are no respecters of property rights.

What does all this show? Well, simply that supporting our beliefs about *all* this or *all* that is far from simple – yet, paradoxically, we typically get along pretty well with such beliefs.

27. A GAZELLE, A SLOTH AND A CHICKEN

 14. INDOCTRINATION: WHEN BELIEVING GOES WRONG

 2. PINTER AND ISABELLA: TETHERING THEM DOWN

19

ADDICTED TO LOVE

Allow me to introduce you to two friends, Leilah and Luis.

Leilah and Luis are like two lovebirds; they are inseparable. Where one goes, the other follows. We knew it would develop that way, for when Leilah first saw Luis – he had flown in from Peru – she could not keep her eyes off him, understandably as he stood tall, proud and handsome. Luis reciprocated her gaze, also understandably, for Leilah is a beauty, with graceful neck, large sparkling eyes and cute curves to the ears. It was love at first sight; and the love persists. Even all these years later, Luis still nibbles at those curvaceous ears; and Leilah walks alongside Luis, seemingly admiring his proud gait, doe-eyed with love. Luis' male friends go cavorting with any Pam, Lynne or Harriet, but Luis remains happily faithful to his Leilah.

Love can have that effect, for better or worse, and, allowing for some literary embellishment, our sketch could apply, in principle, to couples we know. People fall in love – both at first and later sights – and remain in love, though the love may develop in various directions. The puzzle being raised here is whether the sketch above could be truly descriptive of Leilah and Luis, when Leilah and Luis are llamas – or, for that matter, any similar creatures, be they alpacas, leopards, zebras – or voles.

'Voles?' you ask. Voles enter the picture because prairie voles are highly monogamous in the sense of bonding together though not, apparently, sexually monogamous. Once two prairie voles have bonded, they huddle as one, protect each other and stay together, in contrast to the rampant promiscuity amongst meadow voles who lack any pair-bonding.

Discovery of voles' lifestyles generated press reports of the eternal love of prairie voles, so dissimilar from the meadow vole's drive for instant sex and 'I want space'.

In contrast to popularist reports, we need not bind 'falling in love' with everlasting bonding. Let us focus on what it is to be in love – and hence whether only human beings can be lovers. We restrict ourselves to romantic or erotic love; we are not engaging questions of parents' love for their children and campaigners' love for humanity.

Do llamas fall in love?

Now, it is possible for llamas, and other animals, to behave in ways that humans do when falling in love and staying in love. The 'possible' is a logical possibility: there certainly is nothing impossible in two llamas living together as described above, except for the question of whether it really is 'love'.

Looking at love biochemically, we may be tempted to see humans in love as merely more complicated instances of animals' pair-bonding. Scientists speak of vasopressin receptors and their neural location. Prairie voles, unlike meadow voles, have sufficient receptors relevantly located; so, a particular prairie partner is associated with reward, thus explaining the bonding with that partner. Prairie voles become addicted to – 'fall in love with' – their partners, and stay committed. If jack-the-lad meadow voles have their low-level vasopressin receptors increased, they too will pair-bond.

Romantic love has, indeed, been likened to addiction, an addiction grounded in the biochemistry. You meet someone, like them enough to see them again; and, if things go well, you are soon craving their company. As with cocaine, take a little and you crave more. If the lover goes off with someone else, you suffer withdrawal symptoms.

If love is understood solely as such addictive behaviour – and if addictions are explained by the biochemistry – then llamas can fall in love and remain in love. But to see love in biochemical terms may blind us to what love means for individuals. The brain's biochemical traits may help to explain how individuals come to love – as, in myth, do elixirs of love – but they do not thereby show what love is. Knowing that water is composed of hydrogen and oxygen fails to display the wetness of water, its thirst-quenching properties and how we may swim in oceans and be awed by thunderstorms.

If Luis loves Leilah, he certainly is intensely attached to Leilah – and that can be true whether Luis and Leilah are llamas, human beings or prairie voles. Attachment, though, is insufficient to establish love. You may be highly attached to your car, your job and the whisky bottle – but usually it is, at best, only metaphorical to describe you as being in love with them. The attachment of love is intermingled with appraisals that the loved ones are highly valuable and merit concern for their sakes. You may value your car; but you cannot seriously do things to further the interests of the car from its point of view, for it has no point of view. You cannot act for its sake.

Now, a llama does possess a point of view. We humans can value llamas and deliberately do things for their sake, furthering their interests. Luis Llama may behave in such a way that he furthers Leilah's interests. Perhaps he moves aside so that Leilah has access to the better grass; perhaps he stands between her and an attacker. Do such actions, though, show that he values her and is acting 'for her sake'?

Llamas lack the language of evaluation; indeed, they seem to lack language altogether. Some, though, may argue that the relevant valuation and concern is sufficiently demonstrated by what the llamas do. If Luis acts as just described, that shows that he values Leilah. Yet even if that is so, we may feel his behaviour is insufficient to establish love. The behaviour does not show that Luis must therefore be acting for Leilah's sake — deliberately acting to benefit her.

Let us also reflect on some additional and associated features of love.

Many lovers, for example, believe that the love enhances their lives. Of course, they may be mistaken: there are tragic loves. Typically, though, love blossoms when lovers see each other as valuing each other and their loving relationship, and act in the interests of each other. If genuinely in love, Luis values Leilah for her sake; and Luis's attachment is deepened if he then becomes aware that he is valued by Leilah.

Luis's deepening love, when sensed by Leilah, deepens the mutual attachment further.

The desire to be with the loved one, furthermore, is not without reason. Reasons can be given by lovers for why they love being with the beloved. They may be mistaken reasons; they may be very sketchy – but it is unlikely that lovers would hold fast to the claim that they love each other truly for no reason at all.

The puzzle about whether llamas and other non-human animals can fall and be in love, as has been seen, comes down to whether we can rightly ascribe to non-human animals a range of psychological features. The features include being aware of reasons for the attachment, valuing the beloved for their sake, possibly judging that life is enhanced by the love. It is far from plausible to believe that non-human animals possess the capacity, at an appropriate level, to evaluate, to act on reasons and to decide to act in the interests of others. So, there is no good reason to think that llamas – or dolphins or voles – can fall in love, be in love and be lovers, once love is seen as requiring more psychological depth than mere attachment.

*   *   *

We often project our psychology onto non-human animals – even onto the inanimate. We may imagine ourselves in the animal's place, describing the animal's psychology in terms that would correctly apply to us. Why we may think of this as mere projection or metaphor – the animals are not really in such states – is because the psychological states essentially involve beliefs. Now, beliefs require possession of concepts and concepts point to language possession; but, some argue, non-human animals lack appropriate language structures. Hence, they lack many complex psychological states including those necessary for love.

Llamas have pleasures, respond to scents and snuggle up against scent providers, but does this show that they possess beliefs about such matters? Well, perhaps many non-human animals can possess states akin to primitive belief, but it is difficult to see how, without language, non-human animals could possess concepts of reason, explanation, and doing things for the sake of another. And without such concepts, Luis cannot be in love with Leilah. Love may be blind; but not that blind.

20. MERCY: TEMPERING AND TAMPERING WITH JUSTICE

22. THE FROG, THE SCORPION AND 'THOU SHALT NOT'

26. PREFERENCES: AVOIDING THE MONEY PUMP

 ## 14. INDOCTRINATION: WHEN BELIEVING GOES WRONG

20

MISFORTUNE, MISS FORTUNA –
AND MALICIOUS DELIGHT

In the days of duels, let us imagine that a Sir Percy challenged a Lord Walsingham. It was to be a duel to the death. They met at dawn, pistols ready. The handkerchief dropped – the agreed signal – and they advanced upon each other. The noble Lord, nervous, fired two shots rapidly – and too soon. He missed. Sir Percy's pistol glinted under the rising sun as he drew closer. His eyes met those of the man who had so painfully cuckolded him. Walsingham was at his mercy.

Supporters of Sir Percy praised his mercy; for, although he was a fine marksman, his firing merely grazed the noble Lord. Sir Percy had not blown Lord W to his Maker; yet honour was satisfied. Sir Percy's detractors, though, whispered that he was no merciful man at all; he had performed the 'merciful' act in the hope that the indebted Lord would aid his further advancement in society.

Merciful acts are those that are less harsh than they need be, under the rules or assumptions in question. To be properly merciful the actions are grounded in compassion for recipients of the mercy. 'It is a fault to punish a fault in full,' remarks Seneca.

When somebody who has been harmed displays mercy to the agents of that harm, he may also forgive those agents; this may quell his resentment, his anger. Despite that, forgiveness is independent of mercy. Some women may forgive their rapists, but they are rarely in a position to be merciful and, even with forgiveness at heart, they may oppose mercy in the sentencing. Even if Sir Percy manifested genuine mercy for the noble Lord, he may never forgive.

'Blessed are the merciful.' Whether believers or not, people typically view mercy as a virtue, as they do forgiveness. Mercy, though, cannot be demanded: for mercy, we beg. Mercy is a gift which those in authority may choose to bestow, be the authority legitimate lenders with the right to repayments or kidnappers possessing the power to take victims' lives illegally.

That justice should be tempered with mercy is a common thought. To temper justice, though, is to tamper with justice – and such tampering seems to undermine the justness of justice.

Is mercy always unjust?

The puzzle arises from two presuppositions. The first is that mercy, although perhaps to be encouraged, is not obligatory;

it is something that we may choose to give. The second pre-supposition is: justice is demanded and is what people deserve.

Consider two court cases concerning two seemingly similar offences and offenders. One judge, Judge Merciful, shows mercy, delivering a reduced sentence; the other judge, Judge Strict, does not. Merciful seems to offend what justice requires. The sentencing difference also seems unfair. To look more closely, perhaps we need to separate areas where justice should be dispensed from other areas.

Judges should judge on the basis of law, not their personal sense of compassion and inclinations to mercy. The law may permit leniency, if there are mitigating circumstances. The different sentences delivered by Merciful and Strict may in fact rest on some relevant differences. Perhaps Merciful's offender, in contrast to Strict's, was filled with remorse or acted under provocation. The difference in sentences resulted from a finer awareness of circumstances. If so, Merciful is wrongly described as merciful. She and Judge Strict are judging according to the law. The leniency showed by Merciful is not a gift, but a legal obligation.

On the view above, permitted pardons and reduced sentences should not be instances of mercy, but of justice based on close examination of circumstances. If the close examination does not yield justification for reduced sentences, then reductions ought not to be given. Mercy has no place where justice is dispensed.

If mercy, properly understood, has no place in the judicial system, what role may it rightly play in other institutions and individual relationships? School teachers sometimes, with changes of heart, cancel detentions. Parents may relent and, instead of stopping proposed treats because of their children's misbehaviour, they feel sorry, letting the treats go ahead. Perhaps, though, these leniencies, as a result of pity or compassion, are too trivial to merit accolades of 'mercy'.

In case stakes need increasing, let deaths be at stake, with pirates, hijackers and kidnappers seemingly exercising mercy, releasing their victims while still alive – and not because of special mitigating conditions. These serious cases are, though, of wicked acts being threatened and then dropped; so, there already existed moral obligations for the hijackers and others not to go ahead with the threats. Hence, they were not bestowing gifts: properly speaking, they were not being merciful.

It appears that we are left with the relatively trivial cases, such as those cited of teachers and parents; but appearances are mistaken.

Within the context of duelling – and assuming Sir Percy and Lord Walsingham both freely consented – we have a life-and-death matter, possessing the possibility of mercy. To take the well-known example from *The Merchant of Venice*, when Shylock pursued his claim for a pound of Antonio's flesh, Shylock could have exercised mercy as urged by Portia, waiving his contractual right. If I break my promise to repay £100,000, the lenders could take me to court, knowing that it would result in the break-up of my family and my refuge in whisky. They could, though, be moved by compassion: they could exercise mercy and not pursue the claim. In waiving their contractual rights, arguably, the lenders are not thereby being unjust or shirking duties.

The overall approach outlined above is that in formal judicial cases, where justice should prevail, mercy has no place. It has a place where questions of injustice do not arise. And that may seem right.

* * *

Our mercy puzzle may appear to be resolved; but the resolution is too tidy, too easy. Let us return to Sir Percy and his mercy towards Lord Walsingham. We may praise that exercise, but, as noted, Sir Percy was not obliged to exercise thus.

Suppose Sir Percy found himself in another duel, with similar dishonour at stake and similar vulnerability of his opponent, but now facing someone else, say, Lord Willingham. Sir Percy, on this occasion, chooses no exercise of mercy. Has he not now acted unfairly? He showed mercy to Walsingham but not to Willingham. To be fair, he ought to have treated them in the same way. Further, if Sir Percy was right to exercise mercy with Walsingham, ought not others also to exercise mercy in similar circumstances?

Once again, as with our discussion of Judges Merciful and Strict, mercy is losing its flavour of being a voluntary gift bestowed. If it is justified in one case, then fairness dictates that it should be applied in similar cases. Mercy would then be no gift to give, but a quality demanded of us; yet then, paradoxically, it is no longer mercy.

Humans that we are, on occasions we act with caprice: we value exceptions, of showing greater kindness for some over others, despite offence to fairness. That is being merciful. It is unsurprising that we should have such muddles in our lives. After all, we are human – all too human.

29. A KNOWING GOD KNOWS HOW MUCH?

24. EXEMPTIONS: DOCTORS, CONSCIENCE AND THE NIQAB

 16. WALK ON BY ... ?

21

SPEAKING OF WHOM?

We approach this puzzle courtesy of a reduced scene from Lewis Carroll's splendid *Through the Looking Glass*.

'Whom do you see on the road?' asks the White King.

'Nobody,' replies Alice.

'Ah, to be able to see Nobody and from this distance too,' muses the King.

The confusion worsens for, when the Messenger arrives, the King asks, 'Whom did you pass on the road?' 'Nobody,' replies the Messenger. 'Quite right,' says the King. 'This young lady saw him too. So, Nobody walks slower than you.'

'What?' says the Messenger indignantly, 'I'm sure Nobody walks faster than I do.'

'He can't do that,' replies the King, 'Otherwise he would be here before you.'

The White King mistakes 'Nobody' for a name (and hence our upper case 'N'). In order to talk of nobody, there is, though, no need for a Mr or Mrs Nobody to exist.

We talk about non-existent entities – about unicorns, Santa Claus and Sleeping Beauty. Our puzzle here, though, is more fundamental and general. How do we manage to talk about items far away in time or space, or even nearby, yet with which we lack contact? How do we know whom we mean when we speak of Zeno, Shakespeare and Newton? After all, none of us has ever met them.

The quick response is that there is no need to meet items in order to talk about them. That is true. The question remains: how does a proper name, when used, target a particular item? In using the name 'Zeno' we manage to speak of the flesh and blood Zeno, a philosopher who lived many years ago, rather than of Plato, Julius Caesar or Shakespeare.

The next quick response could be that Zeno is whomever we designate by the name 'Zeno'; but that traps us into a circle, for who is that person?

Our puzzle relates, of course, to named towns, sculptures and mountains, but to retain focus, let the question be:

How can we talk about people of the distant past?

An easy answer is that we are talking about whichever person was given the relevant name at the time. That, though, usually will not work. When writing of Zeno in this chapter, Zeno, a philosopher, was being pinpointed, yet there are many other individuals called 'Zeno', including some cats and dogs. True, we may now insist that, given the context, the individual designated is *the philosopher with the name 'Zeno'*. Not even that, though, is sufficient to pinpoint the particular individual in mind, for there could well have been other Zenos who were philosophers – indeed, there were. Witness Zeno of Citium, founder of Stoicism, different from Zeno of Elea.

The approach above associates descriptions, for example 'philosopher', with the name in question. Building on that approach, we may argue that proper names, to work, require associated collections of quite a few descriptions. The descriptions need to be sufficiently detailed to hit one and only one individual. They need uniquely to identify one individual. Whichever item satisfies the descriptions is the item about which we are speaking.

Modifications are needed to the above approach – the 'description' or 'satisfaction' theory – for we may hold some mistaken descriptions of the individuals in question. Further, some descriptions carry more weight than others.

In talking about Zeno, we are here talking about the Greek philosopher, who flourished around 460 BC, who came from Elea, who produced paradoxes of motion, and who was tall. But, suppose such an individual existed satisfying all the relevant descriptions except for being tall. We should accept that we were talking about the individual who was a Greek philosopher, came from Elea, and so on – but were mistaken about his height. His being a philosopher of paradoxes weighs far more than his height – or even his weight.

The historic persons, therefore, to whom we refer are those individuals who satisfy a weighted number of a cluster of descriptions with which the name we use is associated. This alleged solution, though, of names requiring identifying descriptions – and those descriptions fixing the item being designated – has problems.

Here is one problem. Think of the numerous names we use every day to talk of historic characters yet concerning which we lack identifying descriptions. We speak of Byron, of Newton, of Plato – of Zeno – yet many of us have few descriptions associated with the names. Most people probably know of Plato only that he was an important Greek philosopher – but that description, of course, fails uniquely to pick out just one individual. Pupils may gather from teachers' comments the names of Newton and Darwin, yet confuse who did what. Surely, though, when pupils wrongly announce, 'Ah, yes, Newton proposed evolutionary theory', they say something incorrect about Newton, not something correct about Darwin.

The problem just outlined is answered by recognizing that we often defer to experts who have the means for identifying whom we mean. Maybe we know a little about Newton, Plato and Zeno, but when we use those names, we ultimately mean the individuals concerning whom relevant scholars possess identifying information linked to the name in question and some minimal information we have. 'Zeno? I mean whichever one the current philosophical purveyors of paradox usually mean.' We pass the 'meaning buck' to others – and it is those others who hold relevant clusters of descriptions associated with the names in question. This has been termed 'the Division of Linguistic Labour'.

*　　　*　　　*

The satisfaction theory, discussed above, is not out of the woods yet. Here is another problem. Can we not make sense of the experts being wrong?

The expert belief is that Shakespeare wrote *Othello*, *Hamlet*, *King Lear* and so on. That, as is sometimes proposed, could be, or could turn out to be, false. Suppose it is false. When we have been speaking of Shakespeare, have we then been speaking of Bacon or Marlowe or some other writer? We should insist that we have often been speaking of Shakespeare. In discovering the mistaken attribution, we say, 'Ah, so Shakespeare did not write *Othello* and the other plays.' In saying that, we do not mean that the author of *Othello* did not write *Othello*.

On the satisfaction theory, we fix the items about which we talk by clusters of descriptions. But, in most cases, those descriptions just happen to apply to the individual – and hence, they may not apply. Aristotle might not have written any philosophy. He might have been a pig farmer, and, somehow, through historians' errors or deliberate misrepresentations, he was spoken of as the great philosopher who wrote the *Metaphysics*. The very fact that we can make sense of that suggestion shows that, at the very least, satisfaction theories need to be nuanced and handled with great care.

To return to 'nobody' who started us off, non-existent individuals, fictional characters, are in a different boat from historical figures.

We have to identify Oliver Twist, the fictional character, by descriptions – for there is nothing more to Twist than the descriptions given by Charles Dickens. There is no sense to the idea that Dickens may have mistaken Twist's characteristics. In contrast, there is sense to the idea that we could be mistaken about Homer. Maybe Homer, the Greek poet, did not create the Homeric poems, the *Iliad* and *Odyssey*, but someone else did. And we may ice the puzzling cake further, by adding that that someone else was also named 'Homer'.

23. CREAMY PHILOSOPHERS: WHO KNOWS WHO KNOWS ...

25. PIN DROPPING

30. A WHOLE CLOUD OF PHILOSOPHY – FROM *COGITO ERGO SUM* TO A DROP OF GRAMMAR

22

THE FROG, THE SCORPION AND 'THOU SHALT NOT'

FROG: I have a feeling of déjà vu, swimming across the river, with you on my back, Ms Scorpion. I guess I shall come to a sticky end – well, a wet and drowning end.

SCORPION: I fear you're right, Mr Frog; but 'tis kindly of you to be carrying me to the other side.

FROG: Remind me, though: why do you sting me *before* we're safely across the river? It's most odd as it leads us both to a watery demise.

SCORPION: It's in my nature. It's something that I cannot help.

FROG: Never been sure of this tale, often misattributed to Aesop, for it is surely not in my nature to give lifts to scorpions. Still, there it is. If only, Ms Scorpion, you could control your nature …

SCORPION: At least until I safely reach the other side – instead of dooming me as well as you. No doubt there's an evolutionary explanation for these things.

FROG: No doubt – and I note your revisionary thought that evolution should have delivered you a better sense of self-interest, with your reaching the other side before stinging me. But, self-interest to one side, have you not heard of morality, of kindness, of fairness? Of how morally you should treat me well, instead of using and abusing me?

SCORPION: You've been listening to those human beings, haven't you, Mr Frog? Yes, they burble on about such matters – though without much concern for scorpions and frogs – but from whence does that morality derive?

FROG: Good question. After all, we non-human creatures lack any sense of morality. Ah, but we are mere evolutionary products of natural selection.

SCORPION: And humans are not? They're as much part of the natural world as are we. And you're right, Mr Frog: there's no morality in nature. Witness my forthcoming sting.

FROG *[shuddering]*: Perhaps those human beings are right – those who insist that they're made in God's image. Perhaps the moral sense is a spark of the divine. It cannot be a spark of nature, for nature tells us how things are, not how they ought to be.

SCORPION: Forget about divine sparks. Human's moral sense is just another product of evolutionary advantage. If you listen to evolutionists' babble, they increasingly explain how creatures of certain types, possessive of moral concerns, are more likely to flourish than others. Well, their genes are the ones more likely to proliferate.

FROG: You mean that, in the end, acting morally is just natural instinct, accounted for by certain genetic survival advantages.

SCORPION: Yes, a species – and hence its genes – is obviously more likely to flourish, if the members tend their young, help others, and show special concern for close relatives. Even we small creatures do that to varying degrees. And think of ants and bees and meerkats: self-sacrifice appears to happen, but there's no morality there. They aren't judging that helping others is what they *ought* to do. It's just what they do.

FROG: I see. There are no moral *oughts* in nature, even human nature.

SCORPION: At bottom, human kindness, self-sacrifice and appeals to justice, are no more divine, no more super-natural, than my natural instinct to – well, I'm sorry about this – but to sting … *[splash, glug, glug]*

From whence comes morality?

Morality puzzles many people, even those who feel that the existence of the universe has no need for God or gods. The existence of moral truths – of what we morally ought and ought not to do – leads many, though, to turn to a divine source such as the Bible's Ten Commandments: thou shalt not kill; thou shalt not commit adultery, and so forth. In fact, there are many, many more divine commandments, but they tend to be overlooked these days.

Morality, it is judged, is a matter of God, the divine law-giver, telling us what we ought to do. Human beings – in contrast to frogs and scorpions – possess the privileged capacity to understand the divine law. So, the assumption up for challenge is:

If there are objective moral truths, then there must be God who commands them.

With that assumption, the argument goes one of two ways. Either you believe that there are objective moral truths, hence you conclude that God must exist – or you reject God's existence and so you reject the existence of objective moral truths.

Must the assumption be accepted? The answer is 'No'. There may be a third way – a third way between morality as divine and morality as delusion. First, let us look at the divine answer and then turn to whether there is a third way, distinct from the delusion.

Consider the proposal that goodness (including rightness) is what is commanded by God: to say that protecting innocent human life is good is to say that God commands it. The idea is that goodness is determined by some supreme authority which we should obey. The natural question that follows is: how does God determine what is good and hence what to command? Here, we have two possible answers.

One answer is that goodness exists independently of God – and so God, being of a certain character, chooses to command the good. On this understanding, God commands the good because it is good; the good is not good because God commands it. If we follow this path, objective moral truths do not ultimately depend on God. It is therefore possible that we human beings can uncover those truths without any need for God. Certainly, they exist independently of God.

The other answer is that what counts as being good is fixed by God. Whatever God ordains as good is, by definition, good. Were he to command killing the firstborn – allegedly did he not once command such in Egypt? – such killing would be morally good. Were he to command men to treat women as slaves, then to do such would be good. The objection to that line of argument is that it gives an outrageous understanding of what morality could be. The reply by godly believers is, of course, that God could never ordain such things – because he is all good. That reply, though, swings us back to goodness being identifiable as something distinct from God, otherwise whatever God is like would count as good.

Sometimes it is proposed that God is identical with Goodness. This, though, ends up explaining the source of goodness as being Goodness, which is no good explanation at all. If the response is, 'But God also cares about human beings,' then the puzzle becomes how Goodness could have such personalized characteristics.

Tying morality to God, it should be noted, does not help us to know what is good, what is bad. Ancient texts deemed 'holy scriptures' lead to conflicting answers: witness the disputes between religions and within a single religion. 'It is written thus' is no reliable means for discerning morality.

If the divine theory is rejected – we have given only a flavour of the debate – are we left with objective morality as delusion, as outlined by Ms Scorpion?

*   *   *

The proposed third way is that moral truths need be neither divinely grounded nor delusory. Truths exist about climate changes and the Earth's orbit of the Sun. Such truths are objective and independent of what humans think.

Now, it would be most peculiar if, in nature, there existed empirical facts such as 'Killing is morally wrong' or 'You ought not to break promises'.

We should, though, stretch our eyes and minds. Think of mathematical truths, usually treated as independent of human beings, yet not necessarily pointing to God. They are objective necessary truths; yet when wandering through forests, we meet trees, beer cans and rabbits, but not numbers, right-angled triangles and abstract syllogisms. Maybe, as with mathematical truths, moral truths can yet be objective, without divine resort. True, moral truths, unlike mathematical truths, tell us what we ought to do, but that just is their character. True, we are sometimes blind to morality, but there is much of the natural and mathematical worlds to which we are blind.

The many disputes in morality may indicate lack of objectivity, but the disputes usually concern applications of morality; and disputes also arise about the application of mathematics to the world. Many, many people, from many different societies, see that, other things being equal, innocent people ought not to be killed, promises should be kept, and people should be treated fairly. Dilemmas arise when circumstances bring such principles into conflict and when facts are in dispute – for example, whether a human foetus is a person, whether fox-hunting is cruel, and whether you should break a promise if it would ease someone's pain.

In contrast to scorpions and frogs, we are intelligent creatures who can reflect, reason and plan for the morrow:

such attributes provided us with evolutionary advantages. Possessive of intelligence, we can also spot abstract mathematical truths and discern moral truths. Now, the ability to uncover such truths may or may not aid survival. Evolutionary explanations can account for what is advantageous – but the advantageous may carry features unrelated to survival.

There is no doubt an evolutionary explanation concerning the survival value of our having the ears that we have. An added feature of ears is their ability to support the arms of spectacles; but the evolutionary explanation for the existence of ears says nothing about spectacle-supporting functions.

29. A KNOWING GOD KNOWS HOW MUCH?

25. PIN DROPPING

 5. 'BUT IT'S ART, DEAR AUNT MATILDA'

23

CREAMY PHILOSOPHERS: WHO KNOWS WHO KNOWS ...

Allow me to introduce you to the importance and nature of common knowledge by way of a puzzle.

Suppose ten philosophers, attending an international convention, are sitting in a semi-circle at the dining table, having just finished some gorgeous creamy dessert in which they all delighted. They can see everyone's face, except their own. No mirrors, no squinting allowed; and they are not permitted to confer. You are the draconian waiter, gazing at them all. No philosopher knows that he has cream on his lips; he cannot see himself. Just two of them have been messy eaters this time, their lips all creamy; the others, surprisingly, are sparklingly clean. For ease, let us call those with cream on their lips 'creamy'. Naturally, all of them, being philosophers, are perfectly rational reasoners – despite the flow of wine – ready to obey instructions.

You say to them, 'Hands up all those who know that they are creamy.' They can all see at least one creamy philosopher. That there is at least one creamy philosopher is universally known, mutually known. Not one of them, though, knows that he is creamy. So, no hands go up. Importantly, no hands go up, if you ask the question again – and again. No philosopher can work out by reason alone that he must be a creamy one.

Now, suppose the same set-up, except that, before any instruction, you announce, 'At least one of you is creamy.' Of course, they knew that in the first scenario: they could all see at least one creamy philosopher. Your announcement, though, magically it seems, alters what will happen. You now instruct, 'Hands up all those who know they are creamy.' No hand is raised. You make the same demand again, 'Hands up all those who know they are creamy.' Amazingly, the two creamy philosophers, and only those two, do now put their hands up. Your announcement, yet of what they each already knew, made all the difference.

Why did the creamy philosophers now raise their hands?

A philosopher with no cream on his lips can see two creamy philosophers, say Alo and Zeki. He reasons that why neither Alo nor Zeki raised their hands at the first instruction was because they each thought it possible that the creamy philosopher they could see was the only creamy philosopher.

Creamy Alo, for example, can see only one creamy philosopher, namely Zeki. Alo reasons that clearly Zeki did not raise his hand first time because he must have seen a creamy philosopher. But Alo can see no creamy philosopher other than Zeki; so, after the first instruction with no one's hand raised, Alo rightly concludes that he must be creamy. Zeki reasons similarly. Hence, when the instruction comes the second time, both philosophers, having each worked out that they must be creamy, raise their hands.

Your announcement made all the difference. Through your announcement, Alo learnt that Zeki knew that at least one philosopher was creamy. Prior to the announcement, although Zeki knew that at least one philosopher was creamy, Alo did not know that Zeki knew. The philosophers' knowledge of the other's knowledge came about through your announcement. Alo and Zeki both came to know that the other knew that there was at least one creamy philosopher. They possessed knowledge of each other's knowledge to that small degree – to degree 2, namely, knowing that the other knows – and so they could reason accordingly.

Our creamy philosophers' tale has just two creamy philosophers. Assuming your announcement is made, it can be proved that when there are n creamy philosophers, those creamy philosophers will all raise their hands on the nth occasion of the instruction to raise hands if creamy. Without the initial announcement and hence the required level of knowledge of knowledge, no hand-raising occurs.

Try a case of just three creamy philosophers, Alo, Zeki and Bob. At the first instruction, no hands go up, and Bob can see why: it is because Alo sees Zeki, and so, Bob thinks, Alo may think Zeki is the sole creamy philosopher. Bob reasons similarly regarding what Zeki may think. So, on the second instruction, Bob still does not raise his hand – but now seeing that, for example, Alo also does not raise his hand, Bob knows that must be because Alo sees a creamy philosopher in addition to Zeki. Bob now realizes that that additional creamy philosopher is he, and so he raises his hand on the third instruction. Alo and Zeki also raise their hands, having argued in like fashion.

With our creamy philosophers, the public announcement by you, the waiter, starts the philosophers on the path of knowing that the others know that there is at least one creamy philosopher. And we may move further along that path – of knowing that they know that others know that they know – and so forth. Common knowledge possesses, it seems, that feature of possible endless reiterations of knowledge, though, for example, with just the two creamy philosophers, Zeki merely needed to know that Alo knew there was at least one creamy philosopher – and vice versa.

Of course, most of us are not logicians, and none is a perfect reasoner, yet paradoxically in our daily lives we depend on common knowledge or, at least, common belief. It is paradoxical because we are finite creatures, yet common knowledge and common belief appear to enmesh us in potentially infinite reiterations. Here is an example.

In Britain, safety requires us to drive on the left. When, on a narrow road, I see an approaching vehicle, I should steer to the left – assuming that the other driver knows the convention. But not just that – he needs to know that I know the convention. Yet not even just that addition, for I need to know that he knows that I know the convention. And so on ... Without common knowledge, common belief, or at least acting as if we possess such, there would be no language, no social living, and at best (or, more accurately, at worse) we should be isolated hermits living no recognizably human life at all.

*   *   *

John Maynard Keynes told of a newspaper competition in which competitors had to select the six prettiest faces from a hundred photographs. The winner would be the one whose choice was closest to the average preferences of the competitors. In order to win, therefore, a competitor had to choose not those faces which he himself deemed prettiest, but those which he thought likeliest to appeal to the other competitors. They, of course, were all looking at the problem from the same point of view – and so, there are further moves to be made. Let us see some.

To win, do not judge who is the prettiest. To win, do not judge those which average opinion genuinely thinks the prettiest. To win, you must devote your intelligence to anticipating what average opinion expects the average opinion to be about the matter. But, of course, winning is more likely secured if you can move to the fourth level of correctly judging what the average opinion expects that the average opinion expects the average opinion to be about the matter – and even further levels could be sought.

Thus it is that lurking in our social behaviour – in public announcements, in conventions – are the reiterations of common knowledge and belief, though in practice, of course, we get by without infinite iterations. Now, that is puzzling; or would it be puzzling only if we were perfectly rational – only if we were perfect philosophers?

31. INFINITY, INFINITIES AND HILBERT'S HOTEL

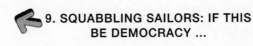 **9. SQUABBLING SAILORS: IF THIS BE DEMOCRACY ...**

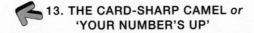 **13. THE CARD-SHARP CAMEL *or* 'YOUR NUMBER'S UP'**

24

EXEMPTIONS: DOCTORS, CONSCIENCE AND THE NIQAB

In some countries and at some times, men and women are conscripted into armed forces, to fight for country and king – for dictator or democracy – yet in some countries and at some times exemptions are permitted on grounds of deeply-held belief. Conscientious objectors may sincerely insist that 'in all conscience' they cannot be engaged in the military.

Catholic doctors, nurses and surgeons – in Britain at least – are permitted to refuse direct involvement in abortion procedures. It is their deeply-held belief that such procedures lead to the destruction of at least potential persons; so they are allowed to discriminate against women needing that medical intervention. Adoption agencies of a Catholic persuasion would ideally accept only married heterosexual couples as adopting parents. The Catholic deeply-held belief is that same-sex relationships provide no proper family home.

Such agencies, though, have received no exemption from accepting homosexual couples as adopting parents. Is there not a puzzling inconsistency?

Sikhs, because of their turban commitment, are exempt from crash-helmet regulations. Employers revise their dress codes so that the religious may wear the yarmulke, niqab, or crucifix. Yet the founder of the International Church of Jediism was prohibited from wearing his hooded head-dress, despite claiming it essential to his newfound religion, and men would usually be prevented from wearing skirts – and women from wearing bikinis – at City meetings. Mind you, perhaps that is not so puzzling: one may doubt the authenticity of Jediistic belief; one may doubt the over-whelming importance to men of skirt wearing and to women of bikini wearing, when in most jobs, serving the public.

Paradoxically, to promote equality – in employment and lifestyle opportunities – unequal treatment is required. Exceptions and exemptions are made, either in law or in practice, usually to accommodate religious beliefs. Yet what moral guidelines are there for permitting some exemptions, but not others? If doctors are permitted exemption from abortion work, why are adoption agencies refused exemption from accepting same-sex couples onto their books? If Muslim women should be free to wear the niqab at work, ought not satirical atheists be free to wear T-shirts displaying cartoons of Muhammad?

We are looking at justifying exemptions from legal requirements and duties of employment, requirements and duties from which normally we should expect no exemption.

What justifies which exemptions for which believers?

A basic ethical intuition is that people should be free to express themselves, so long as not causing unwanted harm to others. The intuition presents an equality concerning respect – though it raises immediate problems. Why, for example, should not some bars, with smokers as employees, be exempt from anti-smoking laws, so that both smokers' and non-smokers' lifestyles are respected? Let us focus, though, on exemptions sought because of people's deep values.

A person's sense of identity may be tied to religious values and belief. 'Asking people to leave their belief in God at the door is akin to asking them to remove their skin colour.' That quip deserves supplementation. Atheists cannot shunt off atheistic beliefs as they enter employment; yet we may agree that the proposed atheist T-shirt above is discourteous, even inflammatory – and inessential to atheists' lack of belief.

The niqab for many (even some Muslims) is provocative and a barrier to an integrated community, when worn within a secular society – in contrast, maybe, to the Sikh's turban or Christian's cross. But when employers prohibit the niqab, some Muslims claim unfair discrimination – their religious views being disrespected – with the resultant lack of employment opportunities that others enjoy. To secure those opportunities, they would need to leave the niqab at the employment door; but the niqab is essential to their lives. How ought we to assess that stance?

According to many experts on the Qur'an, the niqab is not required by Islam; so we may challenge the religious significance of the niqab belief. Muslim women who insist on wearing such dress could therefore be seen as disqualifying themselves from public employments. A response is that some women wear the niqab through family pressure rather than genuine belief: if exemptions are disallowed, then those women would be all the more trapped, having to remain at home. The debate has hence moved into factual matters, judging sincerity of belief and overall benefits for the women.

Exemptions minimally require the 'deep belief' sincerity. Were exemptions permitted, based on mere whims, we could be opting out of numerous requirements, from dress codes to vaccination practices. In societies that value diversity, conformity still has a place – in certain places. Many City offices require high collars and ties on men, while allowing low-cut blouses on women; others insist on modesty in female dress. What is socially acceptable gradually changes, but, in the main, people acquiesce in vast numbers of conventions – until in conflict with deep belief.

The oft-made assumption that a religious basis is required for depth of belief, though, needs challenge. True, religious commitment can afford some evidence of depth, but so too can significant non-religious movements, sometimes for the good – maybe ecological movements – sometimes for the bad, as with certain political creeds.

With deeply-held beliefs, people may sincerely claim that they could not live with themselves if engaging in certain activities. They may appeal to conscience; yet who knows what conscience reports? Were conscience or depth of belief sufficient to justify exemptions, deeply committed racists could use it to avoid anti-racist laws, and misogynist employers to justify paying women less than men. We need something more. For a start, the deeply-held beliefs, the conscience consultations, must not be morally obnoxious.

They must also, even if false, be understandable, as possessing deep importance for the believers. And sometimes they are.

Even the most fervent admirer of just wars may respect people who judge war morally beyond the pale. Even the strongest defenders of women's rights may recognize that abortion poses genuine moral dilemmas. The grounds for exemptions related to war and abortion make recognizable moral appeals to how we should respect the lives of others. In such cases we should at least be receptive to the possibility of exemptions: the deeply-held beliefs are clearly 'other-regarding', concerned for protecting others. Of course, this does not remotely solve the puzzle of which exemptions, whether other-regarding or merely concerning one's own personal salvation, should be permitted.

Circumstances, for example, may be so desperate – too few soldiers; too few doctors – that the relevant exemptions cannot be granted. Practical considerations, though, sometimes boost granting the desired exemptions. Pacifists are unlikely to be good soldiers, but they may give excellent care to the war wounded. Inevitably, competing and practical factors have to be weighed. Of course, some believers, if not exempted, may still refuse to do whatever it is to which they object – they may resign their posts – but, as a matter of fact, practical disadvantages can often cause 'deeply-held beliefs' to be less deep. People compromise, juggling principles with comforts.

*   *   *

When considering how people with different entrenched beliefs can live together, there are bound to be grey areas: people and authorities need to adapt and adjust. Let us return to the adoption agency.

The Catholic concern is genuinely other-regarding: they want what they perceive as best for the children; but homosexual couples may see only homophobia in the Catholic stance. How ought we to view the problem? Assuming a sufficient number of secular adoption agencies – and a society which allows children to be religiously nurtured and taught (highly controversially) how certain sexual practices are immoral – consistency would suggest that the required exemptions for Catholic agencies should be permitted.

In the end, exemptions rest on practical and muddling considerations. This may disappoint some readers, but it is often a mistake to think that there must be a principle that is both right and also determines what should be done on every occasion.

A war criminal's defence is sometimes 'I was just doing my duty'. If the laws are so bad, exemption from duties is no longer the issue: what is wanted is civil disobedience, where we have to stand up and be counted or, in the days of the CND, be counted while sitting down. But let us remember that old texts, just because they have the accolade of 'holy', are not thereby reliable sources for when we should stand up – or, indeed, sit down.

 14. INDOCTRINATION: WHEN BELIEVING GOES WRONG

 22. THE FROG, THE SCORPION AND 'THOU SHALT NOT'

 5. 'BUT IT'S ART, DEAR AUNT MATILDA'

25

PIN DROPPING

Things may be so quiet that you can hear a pin drop; but, for that hearing to take place, you need not merely a pin and the drop, but also a conscious observer to hear. Such a thought should silence the wonder of whether, when trees fall in a forest, there is any sound if no one is present to hear. 'No observer; no sound' may be the principle. If so, the universe is a fine and quiet place, when lacking conscious creatures. Recording apparatus, if magically existing before creatures came to be, would still register the vibrations of those forest 'snaps', 'crackles' and 'thuds'; but, on playback, there would be no sounds to play back, if still no creatures to hear.

There is no good reason to stop at sounds. If no one is present, salt, it seems, lacks any taste; roses lack the scent of roses, and, as for the colours of rainbow, could anything be coloured, if no one exists to perceive the colour? Such considerations led a certain Bishop Berkeley, a powerful

reasoner of the early eighteenth century, to argue that for anything to exist at all, there must be observers, perceivers. 'To be is to be perceived' was the good Bishop's mantra – well, part of his mantra. Perceivers are also beings and yet are unperceived, being not perceivable bodies but minds or spirits; so the mantra in fullness is 'To be is to be perceived or to perceive', with 'perceiving' covering the five senses: seeing, touching, hearing, smelling, tasting.

In speedy summary, material things, themselves no spirits or minds, cannot exist if understood as items unperceived – well, thus argued the Bishop. What we think of as material objects – tables, chairs, mince pies and mountains – are just collections of qualities, of colours, shapes, weights, tastes, softness or hardness; and such qualities depend on perceivers perceiving. To one perceiver, the bathwater feels hot; to another, tepid. The mince pie is salty to one; sweet to another. From one angle, the table looks oval; from another, circular; and so forth. These 'physical' objects are not matter, existing independently of mind – a repugnance, a contradiction, according to Berkeley – but collections of ideas, that is of mind-dependent perceptions.

There need be no worry, though, about tables and chairs popping out of existence when we leave the room (and the room popping out too) and popping back upon our return. We need not fear for the existence of unseen bodily organs and the movements of legs and arms that come and go out of existence, depending on whether they are perceived, be it inwardly or outwardly. There need be no fear, for Berkeley ushers in God, the greatest perceiver, upon whose mind all objects depend. God is all seeing and always seeing. Thus came forth the limerick:

> *There was a young man who said, 'God*
> *Must find it exceedingly odd*
> *That this tree I see, should continue to be*
> *When there's no one about in the Quad.'*

and the divine reassuring reply:

> *Dear Sir:*
> *I am always about in the Quad.*

And that's why the tree
Will continue to be
Since observed by
Yours faithfully,
God.

To answer Berkeley's puzzle, let us resist refuge in God. How may we combat Berkeley's position that tables and chairs, mountains and mince pies are mind-dependent collections of ideas?

Are there sounds in a forest when no one is present to hear?

Can things exist when there are no observers?

To quell Berkeley's argument we should distinguish between the ideas that we have, the mind-dependent entities, and the mind-independent entities that cause those ideas. We sometimes conflate the two because of ambiguous language. When we speak of sounds, are we speaking of experiences or of vibrations in the air? When we speak of the pie being hot, are we speaking of hot sensations or of the pie's molecular motions that cause the sensations? Experiences differ from what the experiences are experiences of. Experiences are mind-dependent; the vibrations and molecular motions are not.

The above is an answer to Berkeley; but Berkeley has a reply. What are the vibrations or motions or qualities that allegedly are distinct from our experiences? One person experiences the water as hot, another as tepid. Which is it? Look at the sky with – then without – rose-tinted glasses: its colour seemingly changes. What qualities do the water, the sky, the mince pies and so on really have? And what do we know about vibrations and molecular motions, save how our senses are affected?

The general point is that our experiences, we casually believe, result from an interplay between the objects and our perceptual apparatus. Our perceptual apparatus contributes to what we take the objects 'really' to be. A cat's apparatus gives it different experiences; a Martian's apparatus (were there to be such creatures) different too. How can we possibly reach out to anything other than our experiences?

According to Berkeley, we perceive just ideas, experiences – and they are mind-dependent. According to others, behind the veil of ideas exist the material or physical objects that cause the ideas. As there is no possibility of lifting the veil even ever so slightly, Berkeley's stance is that talk of such objects behind a veil is idle talk. Mind you, as mentioned, Berkeley does end up with something behind the veil: God. We continue here, though, without God.

*   *   *

The line of argument above can reach a radical conclusion, for my knowledge of other people is based on nothing more than my experiences; so, I am also unjustified in believing other people exist, save as ideas dependent on my mind. I could land in the position of believing that only I and my ideas exist: 'solipsism'. Here, let us return to common sense. Common sense can often help.

Berkeley had us seeing, touching – hearing, smelling, tasting – ideas. That immediately set us on the wrong path. The particular senses need to be treated differently from each other; but, risking the general, we often accept, as a matter of common sense, that we see and touch – and so forth – physical objects. We see the cat, smell the cat, stroke the cat, even accidentally kick the cat. When we see the cat, we have visual sensations; but we do not see the sensations. The sensations, the ideas, are what, arguably, we have when seeing the cat – though we may wonder about the relationship between the cat and those sensations.

If the cat is white, we have sensations of whiteness, depending on lighting conditions. Of course, such visual sensations are lacking, when no one is around to see the cat. Does that mean that the cat lacks a white colour, when unseen? Well, it depends what is meant by 'white'. One quick solution is to argue that an item is white if the following is true: namely, were it to be seen by typical human beings, or maybe discriminating experts, under agreed 'normal' conditions, then the perceivers would have certain visual sensations, namely those of whiteness. Is that visual sensation in the cat? No. Is the cat white? Yes.

The approach, details to one side, seeks to understand qualities such as colours and shapes, tastes and smells, as dispositional: that is, they are understood in terms of which sensations would occur *if* ... When we say salt is soluble, we do not mean that it is dissolving right now: what we mean is that, *were* it to be placed in water, then it would dissolve. When we say salt is white, we do not mean that there are experiences of a whiteness right now, if no one is looking: what we mean, or at least imply, is that, were it to be viewed under normal conditions, then certain visual sensations would occur.

We return to the forest bereft of sentient beings. The winds howl, the trees crash and the lightning is followed by thunder. Were there to be humans present, they would hear those things. So, just as oceans and mountains, shapes and sizes, densities and durations surely existed before sentient beings existed, we should acquiesce in accepting that the deserts were coloured, oceans were salty – and forests were filled with sounds.

Yet does that sound quite right?

30. A WHOLE CLOUD OF PHILOSOPHY – FROM
COGITO ERGO SUM
TO A DROP OF GRAMMAR

 17. LET THE MUSIC PLAY

11. A GOAT WITH GAPS

29. A KNOWING GOD KNOWS HOW MUCH?

26

PREFERENCES: AVOIDING
THE MONEY PUMP

'What flavours do you have?' asks Lucinda, contemplating the home-made ice creams.

'Chocolate, cherry and coffee,' comes the reply.

Lucinda ponders for a moment or two, not exactly happy with a choice so limited. 'I'll have the coffee,' she decides.

The waiter takes her order, but as he turns to walk away, he remembers, 'Ah, we also have plum, peach and passion-fruit.'

'Splendid!' says Lucinda. 'I'll go for the cherry.'

Y

We all have preferences, often different preferences – and what we prefer depends on context, on the options available. Now, the Lucinda story generates a smile of bafflement: how can knowledge of the plum, peach and passion-fruit options lead her preference to switch from coffee to cherry? That seems paradoxical.

That does seem paradoxical; but we can tell a tale and the paradox vanishes. We hypothesize that Lucinda was initially unhappy with going for cherry, but only because it appeared to be the sole fruit flavour available. 'Maybe the ice cream maker lacks expertise in flavouring by fruit,' she pondered. On learning the availability of other fruits, Lucinda gained confidence in the maker's fruity abilities. With such confidence, she could go for her top preference, namely, the cherry – the cherry indeed, but only when other fruits are available. Her preference for coffee gains top place, when only one fruit is available. Context affects her preference between coffee and cherry.

With that background point to the fore, let us see if it helps with some preference paradoxes. First, I introduce 'transitivity'.

If I prefer apples to bananas and bananas to clementines, then I should surely prefer apples to clementines. That is, the preference relation is transitive. Many relations are transitive. If Maynard is taller than Naomi and Naomi is taller than Oscar, then Maynard is taller than Oscar. In contrast to such transitive relations, 'kiss' is intransitive. If Maynard kisses Naomi and Naomi kisses Oscar, it does not follow that Maynard kisses Oscar – far from it. And although Maynard loves kissing Naomi and Naomi loves kissing Oscar, it does not follow that Maynard loves kissing Oscar.

If you are rational, your preferences should be transitive – or so it appears. The classic Preference Paradox challenges the appearance. Suppose the following:

I prefer opera-going with Lucy to attending investment seminars alone, yet I prefer attending investment seminars alone to watching football with Sid. This makes perfectly good sense: I delight in opera and Lucy's company. In contrast, I dislike football and find Sid uneasy company. Rationality suggests that I should obviously prefer opera-going with Lucy to football with Sid. But does it? Paradox arises because I may nonetheless prefer the Sid football option to Lucy opera – and that could be a rational preference. Yet how? Let us set out the question in abbreviated form.

If I prefer Lucy opera to seminars and seminars to Sid football, can it be rational to prefer Sid football to Lucy opera?

Circumstances can be described where the correct answer is 'Yes' and hence where, it seems, preference is not transitive. Suppose that I strongly need to overcome a claim by Sid that I am elitist; and suppose that Sid knows the choice is between Lucy opera and football with him. If I choose the Lucy option, I shall be exposed to Sid's elitist charge. Hence, I choose the Sid option, even though I prefer opera with Lucy to seminars and seminars to football with Sid. Rational preferences, it appears, need not be transitive.

Perhaps the paradox is no paradox at all. Perhaps preferences are no more transitive than 'likes', 'loves' and 'licks'. The problem with acquiescing in this conclusion is the danger of bankruptcy. More accurately, if we have intransitive preferences, then money can, in theory, be pumped from us – until it is all gone – with our gaining nothing in return. It cannot be rational to succumb to that. Here is the money pump at work.

In summary, I prefer opera to seminars and seminars to football, yet, intransitively, I prefer football to opera. Attending opera, seminars and football costs money – and let us pretend the same cost. Suppose that I have a ticket for the football and you hold tickets for the seminar and opera. As I prefer seminars to football, I should surely trade my football ticket for your seminar ticket – and pay you something for that trade, say, £10, seminar attendance being more valuable to me than football. The trade completed, you have the £10 and the football ticket. You still have the opera ticket. I now have the seminar ticket. Here comes the next stage.

I prefer opera to seminars, so I should be prepared to offer you the seminar ticket and, say, another £10, to secure the much preferred opera ticket. I do so. I now have the opera ticket, but am down by £20. You now have the football and seminar tickets and the £20. Here comes the final stage.

Because of my preferences' intransitivity, I yet prefer football to opera, so I should be prepared to trade my opera ticket and £10, for the football ticket that you accepted from me in the first place. The outcome is that I am back to square one, holding just the football ticket, but £30 down: that is not good. You are back with your seminar and opera tickets, and a £30 gain and no doubt a big beam. As you now have tickets that I prefer, you and I should commence trading all over again, with more money pumped from me – until either the money runs out or I see sense, either ceasing to trade or dropping my intransitive preferences.

The money pump demonstrates an irrationality in holding intransitive preferences, unless preferers enjoy loss making. Of course, someone with intransitive preferences, but otherwise rational and resisting bankruptcy, should refuse to trade. But then we must ask what justifies the refusal, for the preferences also provide good reasons to trade. Assuming that rationality does demand transitivity, we are cast back into the Paradox of Preference.

Let us recall Lucinda and her ice cream preferences. We thought of Lucinda as irrational, switching from coffee to cherry, until we understood the relevance of background fruit flavours. In the Lucy/Sid tale, the background, once entered into the preferences, may save me from intransitivity and hence from pumping dangers. Once the preferences are spelled out in greater detail, arguably the puzzle evaporates. Here are the preferences:

First: Opera with Lucy, no elitism displayed to Sid.
Second: Seminars alone, no elitism displayed to Sid.

But if they are unavailable, I may be driven to:

Third: Football with Sid, no elitism displayed to Sid.

Worse options would be: opera with Lucy, elitism displayed to Sid; and football with Sid yet somehow elitism still displayed. Whether I can secure my first preference depends on whether the choice on offer is between football with Sid and opera with Lucy. If that is the choice, and known by Sid, then I end up with my sad third preference – but that is better for me than declining Sid and appearing elitist, opera-going with Lucy.

*   *   *

In the above, we have tied rational preferences to transitivity. What is disturbing is that we hit a new puzzle, when combining individuals' rational preferences, even when individually transitive. Consider an example of voting preferences.

Abe prefers tax reduction to increased overseas aid and prefers increased overseas aid to increased arts funding.

Ben prefers increased overseas aid to increased arts funding and increased arts funding to tax reduction.

Clem prefers increased arts funding to tax reduction and tax reduction to increased overseas aid.

Counting up the preferences of our three voters, we see that tax reduction defeats increased overseas aid: 2 to 1.

Increased overseas aid defeats increased arts funding also 2 to 1. So, given the need for transitivity, tax reduction should surely defeat increased arts funding 2 to 1 – yet it is the reverse: increased arts funding defeats tax reduction, 2 to 1.

Paradoxically, even when members of a group are individually consistent in their preferences, there is no fair and rational means of combining the preferences to ensure no inconsistency can ever arise in the group's preferences as a whole. But should that be surprising? After all, even though separate groups of preferences of an individual may be consistent, there is no guarantee that the totality of that individual's preferences must be. We are, after all, human.

27. A GAZELLE, A SLOTH AND A CHICKEN

 **4. RESOLUTIONS, GOOD INTENTIONS –
AND CREAM BUNS**

 **9. SQUABBLING SAILORS: IF THIS
BE DEMOCRACY ...**

27

A GAZELLE, A SLOTH AND A CHICKEN

Here we have some mixed-up logic – well, at least, some mixed-up thinking resulting from logic – but we approach it by coaxing some mixed-up creatures into a race. There is good reason for this. Our creatures are a gazelle, a sloth and a chicken. So, we have two mammals and one bird. True, this is an unlikely combination. Mind you, the logic will be impeccable.

The race is fair, the creatures positively motivated, no drugs taken. Now, we have excellent reasons for thinking that the gazelle will win. We also have excellent reasons to think that the sloth will come last – she is true to her name – and that the chicken will be in the middle, coming second. Let us set out our beliefs more determinedly.

We firmly believe that the gazelle will win. We know that the gazelle is a mammal; so, a little piece of reasoning leads us to believe that a mammal will win. If we are willing to bet on the gazelle winning, then – were bookmakers to take bets in terms only of a mammal winning or not – we ought to bet on a mammal. If we are certain that the gazelle will win, we must be certain that a mammal will win.

The chicken is a bird and no mammal; so, of course, in believing that a mammal will win, we do not believe that the chicken will win. Now consider:

> Premiss 1: If a mammal wins, then if the winner is not the gazelle, the winner will be the sloth.

Surely we are committed to that claim. If – *if* – a mammal wins our little race, and if it is not the gazelle, then it must be the sloth. After all, the chicken is no mammal. Furthermore, we do firmly believe:

> Premiss 2: A mammal will win.

Therefore, we ought to believe:

> Conclusion: So, if the winner is not the gazelle, the winner will be the sloth.

Yet that Win Conclusion is just what we do not believe. We believe that if, for some reason, the gazelle fails to win, then the winner will be the chicken – with the sloth a very long way behind, slothfully slothing.

Whatever has gone wrong in this simple argument?

Our little piece of reasoning employs *modus ponendo ponens*, abbreviated to *modus ponens*. It affirms a conclusion by affirming the 'if' part of the first premiss. It would be tragic to be forced to accept that *modus ponens* sometimes fails to work. It is the bedrock of our reasoning. Here is a *modus ponens* at work:

Premiss: If there is lightning, there will be thunder.
Premiss: There is lightning.
Conclusion: So, there will be thunder.

The conclusion follows from the premisses: if the premisses are true, then the conclusion is true. Here is more impeccable reasoning.

Premiss: If no umbrellas are available, then if it rains, the guests will get wet.
Premiss: No umbrellas are available.
Conclusion: So, if it rains, the guests will get wet.

However, using similar, seemingly impeccable reasoning about the creatures' race, we reached the paradoxical conclusion that, if the winner is not the gazelle, it will be the sloth. How odd.

One approach to our paradox is to expose an ambiguous use of the term 'mammal' in Premisses 1 and 2. The expression can mean: some mammal or other. We may colloquially say: *any ol' mammal*. The expression may, though, mean: a particular mammal or type of mammal – in this case, a gazelle. We believe Premiss 2 understood as 'A particular mammal, a gazelle, not any mammal or other, will win'. But Premiss 1 is baffling if read as 'If a particular mammal, a gazelle (not any mammal or other), will win, then if the winner is not the gazelle, the winner will be the sloth.' With Premiss 1 baffling us, we have no good reason to accept the argument's conclusion.

Arguably, the above approach fails to solve the paradox. Our belief that the gazelle will win surely supports the more general belief that a mammal – some mammal or other – will win. If I believe that Edgar kissed Elaine and I know that Elaine is a raven-haired woman, then surely I should believe that Edgar kissed some raven-haired woman or other. That latter belief may well be true, even if my grounds for it are lousy because I confused Elaine with Zelda. Zelda is also raven-haired – and it was Zelda who was kissed.

To resolve the paradox perhaps we need to distinguish between an argument's premisses and our acceptance of, or belief in, those premisses. Yes, if Premisses 1 and 2 are true – if those two propositions are true – then the Win Conclusion is true. That is indeed straightforward *modus ponens*; but is our acceptance of Premiss 1 straightforward?

Premiss 1: If a mammal wins, then if the winner is not the gazelle, the winner will be the sloth.

We believe – we accept – that a mammal will win only because we believe that the gazelle will win. So, on the supposition that a mammal wins, if we then suppose that the winner is not the gazelle, we are supposing 'what if' we lack our belief that a mammal wins. If that supposition is consistently applied across the argument's premisses, we lack good reason to believe Premiss 2's 'A mammal will win'. Hence, although the Win Conclusion follows from the two premisses – the argument is valid – that does not justify our accepting the argument's conclusion.

Here is a blatantly extreme example of what is going wrong. Holding fast to our belief that the gazelle will win, what happens if the gazelle does not win? We do not know what to make of that question. It is like asking what happens if the gazelle wins and yet does not win.

The moral of this paradox is not that the formal logic of *modus ponens* is wrong, but that the logician's premisses, conclusions and their relationships are not the same as reasons, beliefs and their relationships. The formalizations of logic are not what they are sometimes cracked up to be.

*   *   *

Suppose we invent a new classification – 'chickelle' – which applies only to items that are chickens or gazelles. We believe that the gazelle will win; so, we should believe that a chickelle will win. Now, consider the following argument structurally similar to our mammalian one.

Premiss 1:   If a chickelle wins, then if the winner is not the gazelle, the winner will be the chicken.

Premiss 2:   A chickelle will win.

Conclusion: So, if the winner is not the gazelle, the winner will be the chicken.

In this example, we do believe the conclusion; but this ought not to be solely because we have a valid *modus ponens* argument with premisses which we believe independently to be true. After all, the mammalian argument possessed such features; but it failed to persuade us of its conclusion's truth.

Why the chickellean argument works is because if we suppose the winner is not the gazelle, we do not undermine our belief that a chickelle will win. In contrast, in the mammalian argument, the supposition that the winner is not the gazelle did undermine our belief in a mammal winning. The mammalian classification was a red herring, so to speak, regarding the argument and the relevant beliefs about the race's runners. The chickellean classification was designed to be relevant.

Arguments are sound when premisses are true and conclusions follow; but whether such conclusions should be *believed* depends on whether the premisses jointly can be believed. Jokes hang on the way that you tell them; what you do hangs on the way that you do it – and belief in conclusions hangs on the way premisses come to be believed.

 **18. TIME FOR ZOOLOGICAL INVESTIGATIONS –
FROM THE BEDROOM**

 **2. PINTER AND ISABELLA: TETHERING
THEM DOWN**

 11. A GOAT WITH GAPS

 **14. INDOCTRINATION: WHEN BELIEVING
GOES WRONG**

28

ON HOW GOOD PUNISHMENT
IS BAD, SO BAD

There is a land, far, far away, where no offences against the
law are ever committed. No, this is not because it is a land
lacking in law. It is not a mis-description of a land where
laws are broken, but remain undetected. The people in this
land – this land, far, far away – are all law-abiding. People
never deliberately park their cars illegally. Tax evasion is
unheard of. No one steals; no one murders. Homes can be left
unlocked without danger; people can wander dark alleys
without fear of attack. This is an ideal land, this land, far,
far away.

This is an ideal land, far, far away, yet its crime-free
status is neither because the inhabitants are naturally law-
abiding, nor because they live so well that none wants for
anything. A few would happily evade taxes, break speed
limits or commit fraud. No doubt a teeny number would

delight in mugging some innocent passers-by for the sheer fun. A few would engage in theft, envious of the lucky wealthy. Some would even delight in smoking while dining out.

Yes, offences would be committed, save that those criminally inclined prefer not to run the risk of detection. This is not because the authorities would be one hundred per cent certain to catch offenders. Likelihood of being caught is, indeed, one highly significant factor in assessing whether law-breaking is worth the risk. The other highly significant factor is the size of punishment if caught compared to the rewards if not.

In the land far, far away, the punishments are severe, extremely severe even for the most minor of offences. Were people deliberately to park illegally, they would have all their property immediately confiscated. Were people intentionally to break speed limits, they would be stretched out on racks for weeks on end. Thieves would be tortured for months and lose various limbs. Murderers would undergo lifetime torment, as would their loved ones. As for smokers in public places, they would be burnt – as were witches centuries ago.

These punishments may strike some as draconian; but are they really, bearing in mind the benefit they bestow? The benefit is the lack of any crime. Furthermore, the punishments never have to be applied. Their severity ensures their lack of application.

What's wrong with this land far,
far away – where there is no crime?

Why do we not have laws and punishment as in the land far, far away?

The answer may seem obvious. The punishments are horrendous: how could we tolerate them? Think how brutal the law's custodians would have to be – torturing, amputating limbs and the like. The answer, though, may itself be easily answered. The sanctions are so severe that everyone aims at being law-abiding. Hence, the punishments are never implemented. We assume – for the moment – one hundred per cent deterrence. Yet even with the assumption, people may still object to the land's penal regime.

Punishment is, said Jeremy Bentham, a mischief. It involves offenders suffering, otherwise it would not be punishment. It is, though, surely wrong to inflict unnecessary suffering. The best punishments, therefore, are justified if causing least suffering, while being most effective deterrents. The authorities of our land far, far away are well aware of that: hence, the severity of the punishments has been fixed to ensure one hundred per cent deterrence. No one suffers the horrendous punishments. What can be bad about that?

Well, it may be replied, the very contemplation of such outrageous punishments is itself morally obnoxious. Even if that reply holds, some morally obnoxious contemplation is a small price to pay in order to live in a land free of crime and free of punishment. Perhaps, comes the new response, the very preparedness to inflict such punishment is so evil that no one would or should be prepared to do so. Again, the reply is how little this evil is – if it is – compared to the gains. Indeed, we may question whether, in reality, there need be any preparedness, in view of the penal threat's effectiveness.

In such a land with such 'ideal' punishment, is there not an highly objectionable feature – one of proportionality? Surely, people who break speed limits do not *deserve* deliberate breakage of their limbs as punishment. What answer may be given by those of the distant land?

Well, do we possess any grip on proportionality? It often is linked to 'an eye for an eye', but few people take that literally. Further, we have no need to worry about proportionality, for the punishments – we are assuming – are not inflicted.

*   *   *

We have been assuming one hundred per cent deterrence. Whether such could be achieved is an empirical, practical objection to the land far, far away. Let us review a little further.

Some crimes are committed when people are in emotional or irrational states. So, even if all citizens are aware of the laws and punishments, sometimes people will be swept along by passions, desperation or madness into breaking the law.

One example would be that of people starving, out on the streets: their need to eat may overwhelm them, and so, they steal. The land far, far away handles that potential problem by ensuring sufficient basic welfare provision.

Welfare provision fails, though, to handle those so racked with jealousy that they murder their partners. It fails to prevent certain mentally disturbed individuals from abusing children. Such cases, though, need not generate punishment. Why? By attending to the mitigating circumstances. Being of unsound mind would be such a circumstance – as, indeed, could be ignorance and failed memory.

Our reasoning above assumes that if people do break the law, then there must be mitigating circumstances; so, harsh punishment – any punishment – is ruled out. The reasoning would parallel the famous catch-22 in Joseph Heller's book, whereby applications to avoid dangerous flying missions on grounds of insanity manifest sanity; so, applications inevitably fail. Well, successful applications – offences – for punishment need to be deliberate and from the sane, but applicants, in applying, lack the right deliberation and sanity, and so applications fail.

We ought not to conclude that people in the land far, far away would therefore break the law, cynically relying on 'unsound mind' defences or similar. For a start, the land may ensure that its citizens are ignorant of the authorities' assumption, or at least unsure whether law-breaking would always generate effective defences against the punishments being inflicted. Further, it may be known that those who escape punishment because of unsound mind find themselves in psychiatric units, a result still highly undesirable.

Of course, citizens may feel insecure, fearing accidentally breaking the law, and maybe fearing the horrendous punishments or the psychiatric institutions, but, even if that is so, is it not a small downside compared to the benefits? Think of the insecurity allegedly suffered by the law-abiding in a society where many crimes – muggings, thefts, gun-crimes – are committed.

∨

The perfect punishment of the land far, far away may appear absurd; yet curiously something similar is accepted by some – *some* – people, namely those who insist that if we fail to obey God's commands on Earth, we face eternal torment. Now, if any punishment is out of proportion, that is surely one. If the possibility of the horrendous punishments of the land far, far away would blight people's lives, then how much more blighted should they be with the fear of eternal torment?

Of course, most religious believers live lives perfectly well, un-blighted, even when accepting the eternal sword of a divine Damocles. Yet a few believers do steal and defraud, harm and murder – as do their non-believing counterparts. Perhaps that suggests that the land far, far away, lacking in crime, is a land of myth, however horrendous its punishments – yet must it be?

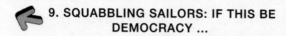 9. SQUABBLING SAILORS: IF THIS BE DEMOCRACY ...

20. MERCY: TEMPERING AND TAMPERING WITH JUSTICE

7. A BOTTLE IMP – FOR SALE

29

A KNOWING GOD KNOWS
HOW MUCH?

'You know – well, I certainly know, being God and a know-all – that you have only given me this philosophical platform to show me up, as swathed in paradox and mystery. Yes, I am mysterious and in many ways beyond human comprehension; so it is small wonder that you human beings judge it paradoxical that I can be all powerful – omnipotent – and so loving, yet there exist so much pain and distress on your mortal coil. But we shall not be engaging that paradox, I foretell.

'And I am pleased, so pleased, that you are not focusing on immoveable stones. Paradoxically, some of you insist, if I can create an immoveable stone, then I cannot move it – and if I can move it, then I cannot create such a stone. Either way, it is argued, I cannot be all powerful. But you humans should

know by now that it is no constraint on power to be unable to perform the logically impossible: that is because the logically impossible is akin to nonsense. People who complain about my inability to deal with immoveable stones should also complain that I cannot blibble, blobble, bleeble. Whatever would it be to blibble, blobble, bleeble, as opposed merely to uttering the words? What would it be to move the immoveable?

'I know very well that you are hoping to make trouble about my knowing everything. Well, go on: see what chaos you can wreak. Of course, I already know how far you will get – because I really do know everything.'

What can God know?

God allegedly is omniscient: he knows everything. That immediately demands the caveat that he knows everything that it is logically possible for such a god to know.

God is usually considered immaterial and without defect; yet, curiously, some believers say that he experiences and knows jealousy and pain, pain through human beings' immorality. It is difficult to grasp how God, a perfect being, can suffer in that way and have such 'personal' knowledge. Presumably, at least, God cannot be scared, dithering or experiencing *schadenfreude*. Perhaps God knows of emotions and feelings in an intellectual, detached way: maybe he can imagine them; maybe he knows how they affect human behaviour. That knowledge would, however, fail to be knowledge in the direct experiential way of humans.

Many people see a puzzle with God possessing foreknowledge. It is sometimes mistakenly argued that if God knows what you will do, then you will not be acting freely. Now, if God knows that you will visit Jerusalem – and he knows this because he determines you to do so – then that could well show that you will not be visiting freely. If, though, God merely knows that you will visit Jerusalem – if he can, so to speak, simply see into your future – then that shows nothing about your freedom.

The error in thinking that God's foreknowledge must undermine human freedom perhaps comes about as follows.

Consider an analogous error. If you are thinking, then it nec-essarily follows – it must follow – that you exist. That is true. It does not, though, mean that if you are thinking, then you exist necessarily: it does not mean that you must have existed. You might not have existed – your parents might never have done funny things with their bodies – and then, of course, you would not have been thinking. We need to distinguish between on the one hand the necessity in a relationship between two items, between thinking and existing, and on the other hand the item, your existence, being necessary. Let us now use the distinction applying it to God's foreknowledge.

If God knows that you will visit Jerusalem, it necessarily follows that you will visit accordingly. That is true. It does not mean that you will visit Jerusalem necessarily – that you could not have done otherwise. If such and such necessarily leads to so and so, it does not mean that so and so is necessary. If the water is frozen, it necessarily follows that it is not boiling; but it does not follow that the water had to be frozen and could not have been boiling. So, God possessing foreknowledge of actions does not mean that those actions necessarily will happen. You can still choose what you will do. It is just that God knows the outcome of your choice.

*   *   *

There remain puzzles about divine foreknowledge, simply because there are puzzles about God possessing any knowl-edge involving time – if God is taken to be eternal, outside space and time. God is often taken so to be, for were he in space and time, it becomes difficult to comprehend how he could have created space and time, a creation difficult enough.

If outside time, it would seem that God cannot possess the type of knowledge that we possess – or, at least, seem to possess – when we know that today's breakfast is in the *past*, that we are reading a book right *now*, and that we shall see Damascus sometime in the *future*. It may be replied that God could have timeless knowledge of such sequences, of how the breakfast comes before the reading which comes before the Damascus trip. Although God could not know, as we may know, that the Damascus trip is future, he could know eternally that the trip occurs in the year 2020. He could know eternally that Spinoza is (timelessly) excommunicated in 1656 and dies in 1677. That is, he could have timeless knowledge of dated facts. The dates are built within the facts known.

Even if God can have timeless knowledge of the sequence of dated events – and we may question God's grasp of 'before' and 'after' – he would still lack the type of knowledge that we possess in knowing that it is *today's* breakfast we have in mind, and that the reading is occurring right *now*. You surely need to be in time to have awareness of what constitutes *now* rather than *then*. That is, you surely need to be in time to have indexical, temporal knowledge, knowledge that is grasped from a particular timed location.

As well as lacking indexical knowledge concerning time, if God is outside space he lacks indexical knowledge of the *here* and *there*. If outside space, God cannot know, it seems, what it is like to see things from a certain perspective, to be here rather than there. He cannot have the knowledge you have when experiencing this book as being nearer than the lamp. Being disembodied, he also lacks the knowledge you have of moving an arm or waking up in the wrong bed.

An eternal divinity, outside space and time, encounters difficulties in grasping human indexical knowledge. Yet we humans, of course, encounter difficulties in grasping God's nature. We have no firm grip, if any grip at all, on what God may be able to imagine about finite spatio-temporal lives or may even be able to do by way of actually becoming human. While God cannot be you, having your experiences, perhaps he can imagine, in some way, what your experiences are like.

It is hard to reach firm conclusions about God's knowledge, for the very concept of an eternal, immaterial, all-knowing, all-powerful being is baffling. Such beings are not regularly met – well, not by many of us. Suppose, though, that there is sense in an all-knowing being knowing *all* truths. Well, all truths must be infinite in number, if only because the number of natural numbers – 1, 2, 3 and so on – is infinite. Conse-quently God's knowledge must be without end. Infinities bigger than the number of natural numbers, though, can be described – see Chapter 31 – and, indeed, it can be argued that God's knowledge must be ever expanding into greater and greater infinities of truths to be known.

We hand back to God.

'Had only you asked, I would have told you straightaway that you shall never grasp the infinite depth of my mystery.'

30. A WHOLE CLOUD OF PHILOSOPHY – FROM *COGITO ERGO SUM* TO A DROP OF GRAMMAR

31. INFINITY, INFINITIES AND HILBERT'S HOTEL

 28. ON HOW GOOD PUNISHMENT IS BAD, SO BAD

20. MERCY: TEMPERING AND TAMPERING WITH JUSTICE

30

A WHOLE CLOUD OF PHILOSOPHY – FROM *COGITO ERGO SUM* TO A DROP OF GRAMMAR

Philosophers have been known to say crazy things; and the following remark, at least in part, strikes many – philosophers and non-philosophers alike – as crazy.

> I can know what someone else is thinking, not what I am thinking. It is correct to say 'I know what you are thinking', and wrong to say 'I know what I am thinking.'

Our Preface gave a little background to the philosophical genius behind the remark, the genius being Ludwig Wittgenstein. Why would he say something that appears so manifestly false? Surely, one thing that I can know is what I am thinking and that I am thinking; and while we often act as if we know what others are thinking, can we ever really and truly know? Can we even know that others are thinking? Let 'thinking' be taken here to guide us to all conscious experiences: sensations, hopes and fears, as well as thoughts. After all, we cannot step into another's mind. 'Other minds', for all I know, with certainty, may not exist.

René Descartes, the early seventeenth-century 'father of modern philosophy', gave voice to the sceptical position, of doubting whether he knew anything other than his own existence and experiences – until he proved (or so he thought) God's existence, from which he argued that the external world and other people do exist: God would not deceive him into thinking such, if there were no possibility of correction. Until he is satisfied of the divine existence, he is a 'solipsist' – thinking that only he and his experiences exist.

Even today in commonsense moods, when we are certain of physical objects, of butter and brains, of mountains and monsoons, we may yet wonder about the existence of other conscious beings. We only ever witness the behaviour of others, never others' experiences. In writing this, I am, of course, assuming that I address other conscious beings: well, maybe – just possibly – a few people are reading these words.

Bertrand Russell's works once suggested that he believed solipsism was true. An American lady wrote to him, saying how pleased she was to learn that he was a solipsist, and how 'I am one too.' If that causes a teeny smile, then we know what solipsism is. Of course, whether the American lady was foolish or satirical – well, that we do not know.

We confront a puzzling conflict, then, between a Cartesian inspired position and Wittgenstein's.

Can I know what I am thinking?

Can I know what someone else is thinking?

Let us approach the first question, thinking in terms of any conscious experiences. Descartes' line is thus: I may be mistaken whether my leg is injured, whether figs, farms and fishes exist – they could be figments of my imagination – but nonetheless I know that it at least seems to me *as if* my leg is injured, as if there are figs, farms and fishes. Over that, I cannot be mistaken.

Wittgenstein's response is that we can have knowledge only where doubt is a possibility. When I am in pain, I cannot start wondering whether I am making a mistake. So, argues Wittgenstein, I cannot know that I am in pain – though I may utter the words as a joke (so much for philosophers' humour) or as emphasis that I am in pain when others doubt me. Nothing more is being said about my relationship to the pain, when 'I know' has been added to 'I am in pain'. Both claims, that I know I am in pain and that I do not know I am in pain – if 'I know' is used in its normal sense – are nonsense. Analogously, it is nonsense to claim that virtue is yellow; it is nonsense to claim that virtue is not yellow – unless the latter makes the point that virtue is not the sort of entity that can be coloured.

When we rightfully talk of people knowing or not knowing things, in the normal sense of 'knowing', it makes sense to talk about their evidence, about what they have seen or heard – and whether they are certain or guessing or pretending. But I do not have evidence for my being in pain – or evidence for my *thinking* about the weather. I may well guess about the weather, but not about what I am now thinking. I may wonder whether my leg is broken, but not whether it is painful.

Of course, 'know' can be used in other senses; but then we need to make those senses clear. When people say with a sigh, 'War is war', they are not making the logical point that war is identical with war. They are expressing a certain feeling of inevitability or hopelessness about war's nastiness.

Perhaps use of 'I know', when in expressions such as 'I know what I am thinking' or 'I know that it hurts', emphasizes my special authority concerning certain of my psychological states. Let us call that the 'privileged' use, contrasting with the normal or 'evidential' use. Wittgenstein and Descartes can now agree that we know, in the privileged use, that we are thinking, that we are in pain – and so forth. The dispute over that question has evaporated. Descartes may, though, have mistakenly thought that he knew, in the evidential sense, about his current pain.

*   *   *

What, though, of the other question? Can I know what someone else is thinking? The sceptical line is that I cannot – but,
once again, we need clarity about the use of 'know'. The evidential use of 'know' requires the possibility of doubt, so my
knowledge of other people's thinking and of what they are
thinking is at least on the cards. Paradoxically, this is so simply
because we *can* be mistaken over such matters. That, of course,
does not establish that we ever do know evidentially what
someone else is thinking, what they are imagining and whether
they are in pain.

Certainly we cannot know, in the privileged sense, what
others are thinking: that is a point of logic. It comes down to
the fact that I, of course, am not in pain in virtue of your being
in pain. Your thinking about Wittgenstein does not thereby
mean that I am thinking about Wittgenstein, with the numerically same thought. But that ought not to lead us to conclude
that I cannot know, evidentially, what you are thinking, or that
I cannot know, evidentially, whether you are in pain. A person
may open her heart to you – so to speak – and you know only
too well what she is thinking, what distress she is undergoing
and what her pleasures are. Obviously her thinking is not
literally your thinking; her distress is not yours; her pleasures
are not yours – though you may be having similar thoughts
and, in a sense, be feeling her distress and pleasures.

'Yet my knowledge of her thoughts and feelings are indirect'
may come the response. But what would it be to have 'direct'
knowledge of her thoughts and feelings? In the evidential

sense of 'know', there is no sense in my even having direct knowledge of my own thoughts and feelings. In the privileged sense of 'know', well, that would be for me to be her, expressing her thoughts and feelings – which is impossible.

These points of Wittgenstein were summarized by him, condensed indeed, as 'a whole cloud of philosophy condensed into a drop of grammar', and by 'grammar' here is meant 'logic'. Yet this may leave us dissatisfied. Even though it is logically impossible for me to be experiencing your thoughts and feelings – the one and same identical thoughts and feelings – I may suffer that impossibility as something missing: 'if only I could get into your mind.'

To feel distress – at a loss – because I cannot be in the privileged position over your thoughts and feelings as I am over mine is to want something as nonsensical as wanting a triangle to have four sides – or as my experiencing a tingle of delight while being unsure if it is I who tingles.

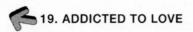 **19. ADDICTED TO LOVE**

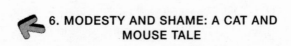 **6. MODESTY AND SHAME: A CAT AND MOUSE TALE**

 **11. A GOAT WITH GAPS**

31

INFINITY, INFINITIES AND HILBERT'S HOTEL

Travelling one seasonally festive day, we encounter some marvellous maids a-milking and lovely lords a-leaping. 'I bet there's the same number of maids as there are lords,' announce I, ignorant of traditional numbers in such festive matters. 'I bet not,' responds my travelling companion.

Bets taken, we could count the maids and lords; but my companion points out that we can, instead, pair the maids and lords off. If one maid or one lord or more are left over, unpaired, we know that the maids and lords differ in number.

The task, easy to do in theory, is not so easy in practice, in view of the leapings and milkings; but eventually we manage – and, sure enough, I lose. We find that some lords are left a-leaping, unpaired with maids a-milking. Clearly, there are more lords than maids. That should be the tale's end, except

my companion, an itinerant mathematician, is bearing a glee-
ful smile, aware of my lack of mathematical skill.

'Of course,' smiles she, 'If you have a group of items and
then take some away, you are left with fewer items than the
original number.'

I readily agree. Even I can see that.

She now directs me to the whole numbers – 1, 2, 3, 4, 5
and so on – and then starts to remove the odd numbers.
I casually remark that the remaining even numbers, 2, 4, 6, 8
and so on, would be fewer in number than the original set of
1, 2, 3, 4, 5 ... The '...' means 'and so on, without end'.

'Caught you!' Her mirth magnified way beyond justification.
'Look,' she says, 'you can pair off all the original numbers, both
even and odd, with just the even numbers – without end.'

The natural numbers	The even numbers only
1	2
2	4
3	6
4	8
and so on ...	and so on ...

'Paradoxically, there are as many even numbers as there are
even and odd numbers together. If both groups, maids and
lords, were each infinite in number, there would yet be as
many maids as both maids and lords.'

I see the point. Although the set of even numbers
contains just *some* of the even and odd numbers, the set of

even numbers is the same size as that of the even and odd numbers combined. My companion has shown this by 'pairing off', 'matching', 'corresponding'. She tells me that two infinite sets are equi-numerous, equal in number, if there is at least some order such that the two sets *can* be paired off with each other, without remainder.

On that understanding, the squares of numbers, namely, 1, 4, 9, 16 … , and the cubes of numbers, namely, 1, 8, 27, 64 … , are also equi-numerous with the positive whole numbers 1, 2, 3, 4 … , as are many, many more series.

'All very interesting,' yawn I, 'but then infinity is endless – so these series are bound to match. You can't have anything bigger than infinity.'

My companion's smirk shows that to be a *faux pas*, a faulty step indeed.

'Some infinities are bigger than others,' she announces. And I am left wondering:

Can anything be bigger than infinity?

The question is whether some number of items exceeds an infinite number. The quick answer is 'Yes'. This was demonstrated by the great mathematician Georg Cantor who developed 'transfinite' mathematics, dealing with differently sized infinities.

Pairing off the items of certain sets and series with the infinite series of whole numbers, 1, 2, 3, 4, 5 … , still leaves some items remaining unpaired. Let us focus, for example, on the decimal numbers – the 'real' numbers – between 0 and 1. They are infinite in number.

There are, of course, the decimals that derive from the fractions one-half, one-quarter, one-eighth … , represented as 0.5, 0.25, 0.125 … There is an infinite number of them. There are also fractions such as one-third, one-sixth, represented as recurring decimals 0.333 … and 0.16666 … These latter two examples clearly have decimals that are endless. There are others, for example, one that derives from the square root of 2, with 1 deducted. This cannot be represented as a fraction: it is an endless decimal: 0.4141 …

Now, pop this infinite number of numbers, in whatever order you like and pair them with the natural numbers, 1, 2, 3, 4 … Here is an arbitrary scattering, with highlighting yet to be explained.

The natural numbers	The decimal numbers
1	0. **3** 3 3 3 …
2	0. 1 4 **4** 2 8 …
3	0. 1 2 **5** 0 …
4	0. 4 1 4 **1** …
…	….

The infinite series of decimal numbers goes down the page without end – and is paired with the infinite series of natural numbers. Whichever decimal numbers you put, in whatever order, there exist some decimal numbers that are bound not to be included. We can spot some 'missing numbers' by deriving them from the highlighted numbers showing diagonally, with a systematic change.

The decimal formed from the diagonal above, if no change is made, is 0.3451 ... That number may occur further down in the series for all we know. But suppose we make the following change, creating an 'extra number':

Whenever we encounter a '3' in the diagonal, we replace it with '1' and whenever we encounter anything that is not a '3' we replace it with '3'.

Our sample extra number starts off, then, as 0.1333 ... We are guaranteed that the decimal being formed is not in the infinite series given, for we know that the 'missing number' differs from the first row's number by having a '1' instead of a '3'. It differs from the second row's number by having a '3' instead of a '4' – and so on, infinitely so on, down the diagonal. We can create more such missing numbers by different replacements. The set of decimal numbers between 0 and 1 certainly has more numbers than the set of natural numbers, even though the natural numbers are infinite in number.

*   *   *

Differently sized infinities seem highly paradoxical; but we should remember that we are talking of abstract entities and ways of comparing them. After all, in the realm of chess, the bishop moves only diagonally; yet that tells us nothing about bishops in life and nothing about how wooden pieces labelled 'bishops' can be physically moved. Yes, infinity does have application to the world. It also has misapplications. Let us see, by returning to infinities that are the same size as the whole number series, 1, 2, 3 ...

Here is Hilbert's Hotel, introduced by the brilliant mathematician David Hilbert. It has an infinite number of rooms, numbered 1, 2, 3 ... Every room is occupied.

A traveller arrives. Paradoxically, he can still be accommodated, insist mathematicians of the infinite. Room 1 occupant is moved to Room 2, Room 2 occupant to Room 3 – and so on – for there is always a higher numbered room to move any occupant you care to mention. Room 1 is now available for the traveller.

Even if an infinite number of travellers arrive, accommodation is no problem. Room 1 occupant moves to 2; Room 2 occupant to 4; Room 3 occupant to 6; and so forth – leaving the infinite number of odd numbered rooms free for the travellers.

It is, though, baffling to describe a hotel with *all* rooms occupied, yet which takes new guests. With the infinite, 'all' and 'size' need to be understood differently from normal. As for making sense of an 'infinite hotel' ...

Imagine meeting a weary Stephanie, walking the last few yards of a mile-long race. She started 1,760 yards away; and is panting the final yards: 3, 2, 1. That is fine; but it would surely be nonsense to think of Stephanie – or anyone – as having started an infinite number of yards away, now sighing out the final 3, 2, 1.

It is not a mere medical limitation that we cannot finish walking an infinite number of yards. It is not a mere architectural and material difficulty that prevents our building Hilbert's Hotel. And arguably it is not all that surprising that abstract infinite series generate paradoxes if applied to the world of hotel rooms, maids a-milking and lords a-leaping.

 **7. A BOTTLE IMP – FOR SALE**

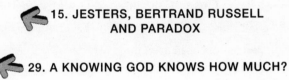 **15. JESTERS, BERTRAND RUSSELL AND PARADOX**

 **29. A KNOWING GOD KNOWS HOW MUCH?**

32

LIFE WITHOUT END: TOO MUCH OF A GOOD THING?

You can have too much of a good thing, or so it is said; but, when the good thing is life, many would cherish the much – and much, much more than even the much. Many would seek immortality. More accurately, many wish for the *possibility* of immortality, of living forever, of eternal life.

The desire for immortality need be no religious yen for a timeless disembodied existence, but rather a focus on the forever as a well-embodied immortal life, down here on Earth or planetary successors. Of course, things could go so disastrously badly that even those most intoxicated with living may wish for no more; but, assuming disasters unrealized, many yearn for more life, not less, and many would see no reason why that more should not be infinitely more. An infinite life is a life without end, and that is what many desire.

☟

'I wish I could live forever.'

Fliss is enjoying her life; she has no good reason to think things will go badly. She is intelligent, attractive, emotionally composed, with high earnings. All is well. 'If only my life didn't have to come to an end. If only I didn't have to cease to be,' sighs she.

'Drink, then, of my life-sustaining elixir,' mumbles the craggy-faced old man, sitting in the dusts of a Mongolian market, possessor of few teeth and to whom soap seems unknown. He points to a potion, as he eyes Fliss, clearly a tourist now off the well-beaten track.

Being a woman of sense, Fliss would right now be dismissing the old man as a crank, a salesman of snake oil, with a potion worthless or worse – but this is a tale of mine and, in this tale, the craggy-faced ancient is no crank and Fliss knows that the offer is genuine. It is, after all, possible that one day, through genetic engineering and medication, humans could be made immortal. Well, it is no obvious contradiction.

'A great idea,' beams Fliss, 'but why haven't you taken it yourself?'

'How do you know that I haven't?' comes the reply.

'But I don't want immortality if I'm going to become exceedingly old and infirm – and with few teeth and no soap.'

'Rest assured, the potion gives you eternal life guaranteed always at your age when drinking. You'll continue at age twenty-seven forever, if that is what you want.'

Fliss, flattered by the 'twenty-seven', quickly establishes that she would not be trapped with the immortality if she changed her mind centuries ahead. With the elixir, she would be receiving antidote pills which cancel the elixir's effects. And so, enthusiastically, having handed over payment, she drinks. Now, the question is, will Fliss at some stage take the antidote? Must not a time come when, if rational, anyone would have had enough of life?

Could immortality ever be good for us?

People often have strong immediate responses to the value of such earthly immortality. For many, it is obvious that a never-ending life at least *could* be good for the subject, the one who lives on; for others, the opposite is obvious. To evaluate such responses, some ground needs clearing with regard to both the immortality and the surviving subject.

A never-ending life could be one in which we are unconscious, in deep dreamless sleep without end. That would give people neither what they want, if they seek immortality, nor what they fear, if they seek avoidance. The life sought, or to be avoided, is a life which contains consciousness, presumably, with some psychological continuity running within. That does not mean that immortal beings, to have valuable immortality, need remember everything; but minimally they require some self-awareness as continuing persistent selves, with memories and projects. Anything less would not be in the spirit of what Fliss, our immortalist, craves.

A never-ending life could be conscious enough, but with its endlessness resulting from an endless recurrence of the same events: you live your life again and again, from zero to age eighty, unaware of the repetition. Such an infinite life is not what is typically sought, when people desire immortality.

The immortality desired is one in which we are conscious of ourselves as continuing to live on and on, undergoing different experiences – presumably, we know we are immortal – yet still being ourselves, our mysterious selves. Now, which questions arise?

One question is whether the elixir protects us from death by accidents and illness – and whether it saves us from significant harms. If it does, then an immortal life would be very different from the mortal. We should lack many worries about dangerous roads, nuclear war, and dying from starvation. Deployment of concepts such as 'courage' and 'safety', and our concern for others, would be very different. For that matter, our blood, bones and organs would need to respond very differently to radiation, high-level impacts and excess alcohol. Our life would scarcely be recognizable as human.

Another question concerns the numbers involved. If I am the sole immortal, then I shall see friends come and go in life; I shall go through the gamut of relationships with different people – and maybe eventually with no people at all, just fading memories of them. If, though, I and a few others are immortal – maybe those wealthy enough to afford the elixirs – would we not be akin to a species different from regular humans? And if numerous people are made immortal, then the eventual 'lack of space' for newly created people suggests relationships between man and woman would eventually be altered: desires for children would need radical revision.

Lack of space prevents detailed review of possible immortalities and their human impact; but key reflections touch tedium and motivation.

If I retain sufficient memory to make sense of myself as continuing, then, after millions of years, would I not be bored by having yet again to start up relationships with new people, if in the world where I am the sole immortal? And if I am in the world where we all are immortal, would I not be bored by meeting the same people eternally?

In response, maybe there are some worthwhile pleasures that could be repeated infinitely, or maybe we would possess the capacity to devise endlessly new projects. If, for example, I am fascinated by numbers, my infinite time could be filled with further reflections on yet higher numbers and their properties: there is no end to numbers. Or maybe, as in a drugged haze, I could value the same heightened sensations returning eternally, or listen to the same music – the same Bartok string quartets – literally endlessly. Or could I?

Even if the boredom and horror can be avoided, there remains a problem for motivation. If something can be put off until tomorrow, why not put it off? There would be an infinite number of 'tomorrow's – so there would be little urgency to engage in anything today. Indeed, with no end in view, unless we repeatedly deceive ourselves into thinking otherwise, we may rightly wonder what structure could be given to our lives. Paradoxically, although many people view life as meaningless if ending in the finality of death, it may be eternal life that endangers meaning and engenders meaninglessness.

*   *   *

For life to have meaning, arguably it needs an end: it needs death to provide a framework within which to pattern our lives. That does not imply that current lifespans are ideal. Perhaps lives of a thousand years would or could be good. Our wave at puzzles is merely to challenge the casual assumption that an eternal life could be a valuable life. We may question how a life can be judged as desirable or not, if we lack conception of its end; and we may wonder what sense there is in its being 'me' living immortally, given the radical difference between a life mortal and one immortal.

Our wave above also provides excuse for display of a logical point.

There is a difference between always wanting something to be so and wanting that something always to be so. Suppose that every day I have a choice between immediate death or an extra day's life. Every day I choose to live for the extra day – hence, I would live forever – yet I may well not choose to live forever. Perhaps we always yearn for the possibility of the extra day; yet maybe most of us know that what we do not want – if sense can be made of it – is the possibility of our life continuing for all days, without end. Bad things, of course, we want to end; and, odd as it may seem, good things really do need to come to an end.

33. MINDFUL OF BARBARIANS – WITHIN AND WITHOUT

 31. INFINITY, INFINITIES AND HILBERT'S HOTEL

 **7. A BOTTLE IMP – FOR SALE**

33

MINDFUL OF BARBARIANS – WITHIN AND WITHOUT

When you draw close to the end of a project – a university course, a life, a book – you may be tempted to step back. Philosophers, as they mature – as the hair greys, eyesight fades and the mind's agility lessens – they too step back. They may gaze at life as a whole, at the value of philosophical reflection in total; and they gaze with the sight of the wise, as if maturity sweeps off those youthful veils that shrouded how things really are and ought to be. Probably though, it is no deep wisdom at all, but merely a sigh at the surroundings, a weariness of the world.

In world-weariness, surely not wisdom, I raise the puzzle of the Barbarian. The term derives from the 'blah, blah', the sheep's 'baa baa', which struck the ears of ancient Greeks when foreigners babbled, ignorant of the language of the civilized, the language of the Greeks. Barbarians could be powerful, prosperous, successful in battle; but they lacked something. They lacked civilization, Greek culture, at its finest.

Barbarians are often outside city walls. They are without. Today, as maybe always, they are also within – within the city, even within ourselves. The barbarous character can be promoted by society: by its laws, structures and those in power. It can be manifested in the Zeitgeist, the attitudes, the spirit of the times.

What do you sense as barbarous – deep down – in society? If that question sounds negative, reflect on what is needed for a good life, a civilized life. What corrupts the good life? To voice the puzzle in our barbarous terms:

Who are the Barbarians now?

The good life, the civilized life, is enhanced by competitive and technological advance. Although we may dream of simple lives unencumbered by scientific success, for many of us our water on tap, light at night, anaesthetics and welfare provision are bounteous boons. They permit time for reflection, for literature, for the arts. Yet we know full well that the advance also promotes the barbarous, the vulgar, the low. Audiences are targeted; artists are big business – and education seeks economic impact. We also know that societies and people that are materially poor can possess refinements and sensualities that we often lack. They may be sensitive to subtle changes in the sky, the weave in the mat; they may gain insight from myths and traditions.

Some barbarities in our society immediately strike home: unprovoked aggression, selfishness, expectations fuelled by commercialism, blaming others when things go wrong. Let us take aim at some underlying ideas.

Barbarians are materialists, in the popular sense of the term. Materialism involves increasing self-centred consumption, with ever more expectations. As resources permit, even fail to permit, Barbarians flaunt gold watches, designer clothes and bigger cars. They seek to acquire more – maybe to drink more, to engage in sex more – as competitive activities lacking imagination, lacking refinement. Nothing better takes hold. Quantity and immediacy swamp quality and taste, reflection and deferment. Contemplation of the sky's colours, the Venetian basilicas or the Louvre's art gives way to snapping more photographs, another sight to squeeze in, while ticking off shopping lists *en route*.

To correct for materialism, some embrace religion. Scripture usually discourages self-centred excess; scripture can lift eyes to the spiritual. Yet certain religious believers sleep too easily with another barbarism – the imposition of belief – forcing their 'good life' on others, through, for example, en-veiling women or criminalizing extra-marital sexual relations.

Unquestioning conformity is a barbarism, be it derived from religious stances or political ideologies. Fortunately, we need not be religious to resist conforming to materialism's vulgar excess. Belief in God is not necessary for us to appreciate the flutter of autumn leaves, the glide of musical phrases, the graceful curve of a neck or to sense the needs of others – or even to value certain scriptural reflections. Note, only 'certain': some scriptural readings merit strong rejection.

*   *   *

Barbarians may be nourished by the *nothing but*. Physical reductionism, scientism – a 'materialism' different from the above – understands love, aesthetic appreciation, our sense of awe before crashing oceans and darkening skies, as 'nothing but' neurological states, states explained by chemical changes and evolutionary psychology. Scientism can mistakenly lead to barbarous devaluations of love, beauty – even, paradoxically, the quest for truth – with conclusions drawn that all we can and ought to do is satisfy our desires. Of course, if scientism really does undermine values, it also undermines Barbarians' valuations that favour self-interest.

We should challenge the reductionist claim, the scientism. There are no scientific laws that speak of awe, beauty and the quest for truth. There are no laws of prettiness, portmanteaux and petticoats. True, explanations may be given of the origins of sensitivity, awe and refinement, but their present existences are not thereby other than they seem. Today's ice remains cold and hard, although, as we now know, constituted by hydrogen and oxygen atoms formed in earlier times.

'Tis better to be a dissatisfied Socrates than a satisfied pig.

Thus wrote the eminent Victorian, John Stuart Mill. Barbarians who embrace materialism in the popular understanding, or who misunderstand scientism's consequences, follow ways of the metaphorical pig. Mill, in swinish rejection, lifts eyes to higher pleasures and improved characters: pleasures of poetry, music, nature; characters of nobility, compassion and honesty. Once educated in the higher pleasures, we recognize their superiority – well, so Mill reasoned. Of course, Mill may be wrong. There is room to argue, reason and reflect about life's values. Such argument, reasoning and reflection, though, already distinguishes those who do so from Barbarians.

It is best to resist 'pleasure' as a label for our aims. Pleasure is not the measure: well, it ought not to be. A better expression, from the ancient Greek *eudaimonia*, is *flourishing*. Mill at heart – and many others – promotes the good life, the happy life, as the flourishing life. Satisfactions of lust and sex, of food and drink, even of sloth and *schadenfreude*, can, though, be nuanced with sensitivities and excellences – seemingly overlooked by Mill. Such satisfactions may feature in flourishing lives just as opera, the sublime art, may.

Flourishing lives need also to be embraced reflectively, and authentically, as truly 'ours', with imagination and perceptivity – and typically with arms outstretched to others. Of course, such lives run risks: things go wrong. Here we meet another barbarism: the expectation that things should always go well, the conceit that we deserve comfortable lives, and the demand for compensation when things go badly.

Knowing the price of everything and the value of nothing: that quip sums up some barbarisms. Barbarians are burdened by increasing desires for so-called 'goods'; they even welcome the burden. Bent under the burden, their eyes are downcast, closed to uplift and enhancement, closed to the refinements, sways and nuances possible in the seemingly mundane as well as the exotic.

*   *   *

In C. P. Cavafy's 'Waiting for the Barbarians', those who waited eventually came to realize that there were no barbarians without. As a result, they fell into confusion.

Paradoxically, what we may need for flourishing lives are the Barbarians, to keep us on guard, to cause our eyes to quest for finer things, saving us from collapse into self-barbarity. Puzzlingly – unhappily, even – we should perhaps parade gratitude to the uncouth, to those with big guzzling cars, even to 'artists' who display nothing but flashing lights or dishevelled beds as aesthetic achievements. Barbarians have their place without – though, ideally, not within us.

> *And now, whatever would happen to us without the Barbarians?*
> *Those people – they are a solution of sorts.*

❯

With Cavafy in mind – that 'Greek gentleman in a straw hat, standing absolutely motionless at a slight angle to the universe' – we may be reminded of what we knew all along: that we too can stand at a slight angle to the universe, with our own perspective, our own take, on the surrounding landscape of nature and humanity, of ideas and the arts – on the friend to whom we wave, the unknown woman who smiles, the memories, music and humours that convey intimacies once shared. And thus it is that we gain a perspective on our life and the lives of others. That perspective may be aspiring and inspirational; it may be resigned and melancholic, serious or whimsical, rational or sensual, stable or changing. It may paint the heavens – or dwell on Earth, aware of limits and inevitable losses. Yet, whichever mixture – it is our own, our own genuine take on life.

And in reflecting and refining our perspective, our embrace, on the world – and the embrace by others – we resist the Barbarian. That is what it can be to be human. That is what it is to be …

> *a Greek gentleman in a straw hat,*
> *standing absolutely motionless*
> *– at a slight angle to the universe.*

APPENDIX 1

FURTHER READING

Complementing this selection of perplexities are my two earlier collections, namely *Can a Robot Be Human? 33 Perplexing Philosophy Puzzles* and *What's Wrong with Eating People? 33 More Perplexing Philosophy Puzzles* (Oxford: Oneworld, 2007/2008).

Philosophical perplexities historically assessed, with lightness of touch, are in the splendid Roy Sorensen's *A Brief History of the Paradox* (New York: OUP, 2003). For some humour and paradox, try John Allen Paulos, *I Think, Therefore I Laugh* (New York: Columbia University Press, 2000). As ever, recall Lewis Carroll, *The Annotated Alice*, 2nd ed., with notes by Martin Gardner (London: Allen Lane, 2000) for the two thought-provoking Alice phantasies.

Michael Clark's *Paradoxes from A to Z*, 2nd ed. (London: Routledge, 2007) is a good, accessible survey of the more formal paradoxes. See also Nicholas Rescher, *Paradoxes: Their Roots, Range, and Resolution* (Chicago: Open Court, 2001) and, for even more, Glenn W. Erikson and John A. Fossa, *Dictionary of Paradox* (Lanham, MD: University Press of America, 1998). R. M. Sainsbury, *Paradoxes*, 3rd ed. (Cambridge: CUP, 2009) offers detailed assessment of some central ones. For philosophy more generally, try Simon Blackburn, *The Big Questions: Philosophy* (London: Quercus, 2010) and note the valuable online *Stanford Encyclopaedia of Philosophy*. Various links are available from www.petercave.com.

Saul Smilansky, *Ten Moral Paradoxes* (Oxford: Blackwell, 2007), tells it as the title says. My *Humanism: a Beginner's Guide* (Oxford: Oneworld, 2009) offers brief outlines of moral theories and dilemmas. For far more: Hugh LaFollette, ed., *The Blackwell Guide to Ethical Theory* (Oxford: Blackwell, 2000).

My own, slightly more academic work, touching on more than just the formal paradoxes, with many references, though still with whimsy, is *This Sentence Is False: An Introduction to Philosophical Paradoxes* (London: Continuum, 2009), hereafter *TSIF*.

APPENDIX 2

NOTES, SOURCES AND REFERENCES

Note: to reduce clutter, when major works are readily available in many editions or online, publication details are omitted. Frequently cited works have their details in 'Further reading' above.

Preface and acknowledgements

The medical motto is Wittgensteinian: the formulation given may be Herbert Feigl's, from the early twentieth-century's Vienna Circle's 'logical positivists'.

The Russell/Moore tale reduces to the classic 'I am lying': see Clark, Sainsbury and *TSIF*. The Wittgenstein/Johnson tale, 'fruit or nut', and other Cambridge reflections appear in my 'Weavings', *A Book of King's*, ed. Karl Sabbagh (London: Third Millennium, 2010). For Johnson, undeservedly little-known, see Stuart Brown, ed., *Dictionary of Twentieth-Century British Philosophers* (London: Continuum, 2005). Ardon Lyon gave the wise reply regarding the Lewy question.

Quotations. Wittgenstein's 'bewitchment': *Philosophical Investigations* §109; 'citizen': *Zettel* §455; Nietzsche's: *The Gay Science*, §341.

The logical puzzle, spotted by John Shand, is from *Scientific American Mind*, December 2009, albeit my example. The correct answer is 'Yes'. Penelope is either a philosopher or not. If she is, then she, a philosopher, is in love with a non-philosopher. If she is a non-philosopher, then Osbert, a philosopher, is in love with a non-philosopher.

Chapter 1 Someone else will ...

D. H. Lawrence's injunction was in response to Benjamin Franklin. For rejection of consequentialism – and stress on integrity – see Williams in J. J. C. Smart and Bernard Williams, *Utilitarianism: For and Against* (Cambridge: CUP, 1973). For later comments: J. E. J. Altham and Ross Harrison's collection on Williams, namely, *World, Mind and Ethics* (Cambridge: CUP, 1995). Utilitarianism is famously associated with Jeremy Bentham and John Stuart Mill. Bentham still sits in University College London. For anguishes and principles, heightened by music and production, try certain operas: for example, English National Opera's productions of John Adams's *Doctor Atomic* and Philip Glass's *Satyagraha*.

Chapter 2 Pinter and Isabella: tethering them down

Tethering and statues are from Plato's *Meno*, Pinter from Anthonia Fraser's *Must You Go?* (London: Weidenfeld & Nicolson, 2010). Carl Ginet supposed drivers hitting lucky in seeming knowledge by spying the only genuine barn in fields of fake barns. For building on true justified belief, try G. S. Pappas and M. Swain, eds. *Essays on Knowledge and Justification* (Ithaca: Comell University Press, 1978). F. P. Ramsey emphasized reliability: *The Foundations of Mathematics and other Logical Essays*, ed. R. B. Braithwaite (London: Kegan Paul, 1931).

Chapter 3 The violinist: should you unplug?

Judith Jarvis Thomson first told of the violinist, in an abortion context: see her paper in Peter Singer, ed., *Applied Ethics* (Oxford: OUP, 1986). Many casually concluded that a woman's right over her body was paramount. Thomson's point was that morality extends beyond rights. For detailed Bentham, see Ross Harrison, *Bentham* (London: Routledge, 1983).

Chapter 4 Resolutions, good intentions – and cream buns

Weak will is discussed in Plato's *Protagoras*, 351–8 and Aristotle's *Nicomachean Ethics*, 7. A recent approach is John Searle's *Rationality in Action* (Cambridge Mass: MIT Press, 2001). Moral weakness is summed by Ovid as 'I see and approve better things, but follow worse.' As E. M. Forster pops up in later chapters – on democracy and barbarians – let us mention his comment relevant here: 'If having to choose between betraying my friend or my country, I hope I would have the guts to betray my country.' The comment also pertains to the 'integrity' matter of Chapter 1.

Chapter 5 'But it's art, dear Aunt Matilda'

Jerrold Levinson, ed., *Aesthetics and Ethics* (Cambridge: CUP, 1998) offers good readings. In Chapter 33, we meet Cavafy who was influenced by 'art for art's sake', yet here, in contrast, Eric Gill attempts 'to destroy the morality that is corrupting us all'. Some saw Gill's sculptures as sexually depraved; others saw them as deeply religious. On what we say about ourselves: well, dog ownership can say something about the owners; and, in the case of vicious dogs, it is something that it is better not to say – and better still not to have such ownership.

Chapter 6 Modesty and shame: a cat and mouse tale

Shame was highlighted by Richard Moran's *Authority and Estrangement* (Princeton: Princeton University Press, 2001). Moran used Kingsley Amis's *That Uncertain Feeling*, where a rakehell (rake, dissolute man) feels ashamed. The Modesty Paradox links to Moore's Paradox: see *TSIF*. Socrates, as gadfly, occurs in Plato's *Apology*.

Chapter 7 A Bottle Imp – for sale

'The Bottle Imp' (1891) is a short story by Robert Louis Stevenson. How far we should gaze into the future does indeed give rise to investment and probability paradoxes. The Charitable Trust puzzle was brought to the world by Cliff Landesman's 'When to terminate a charitable trust?' in *Analysis* (Oxford: Blackwell, 1995).

Chapter 8 Going for cover – from arms dealing to casting couches

Blackmail is raised in Smilansky. Many apparently acceptable activities in capitalism – where things will be done, 'unless' – seem remarkably similar to the unacceptable blackmail. Smilansky investigates a couple of good examples.

Chapter 9 Squabbling sailors: if this be democracy ...

For Plato's analogy and assessment, see Renford Bambrough, 'Plato's Political Analogies' in P. Laslett, ed., *Philosophy, Politics and Society: Series 1* (Oxford: Blackwell, 1973). My *Humanism* looks at democracy and the secular state. For history and philosophy of democracy, see Ross Harrison, *Democracy* (London: Routledge, 1993). Democracy is famously said to be the worst form of government – except for all the others. In Britain there is eagerness for the second chamber – the House of Lords – to be democratically elected. Wisdom would recommend a second chamber Plato-style, with experts from different walks of life, owning powers to check the democratic deliverances that result from persuasive party machines and short-term electoral popularities.

Chapter 10 Misfortune, Miss Fortuna – and malicious delight

Philosophers say little about *schadenfreude*; but see John Portmann, *When Bad Things Happen to Other People* (New York: Routledge, 2000) and Nietzsche's *Daybreak*, §224. Machiavelli speaks of Fortuna in *The Prince* (published in the early sixteenth century). Fortuna, he says, is a fickle woman who deserves to be beaten – and who likes virile young men.

Machiavelli would no doubt be a little wary of expressing his views in such terms today. My thanks go to Sophie Bolat for stimulating thoughts on this chapter.

Chapter 11 A goat with gaps

For sensible survey, see Ardon Lyon, 'Personal Identity' in G. H. R. Parkinson, ed., *An Encyclopaedia of Philosophy* (London: Routledge, 1988). For unity, see Ian Hacking in Harry G. Frankfurt, ed., *Leibniz* (New York: Doubleday, 1972). Physicists apparently accept that electrons can jump, with no spatial continuity, from one location to another – though what is it that makes the 'jumped' electron numerically the same as the earlier – or just a similar one? Does much hang on the answer?

Chapter 12 What sort of children should there be?

See Jonathan Glover, *Choosing Children* (Oxford: OUP, 2006). Harms and benefits are identity dependent: we need individuals to have the 'foothold of existence' to quote the undeservedly little-known Henry Salt. For future people, see Derek Parfit, *Reasons and Persons* (Oxford: OUP, 1984). For non-existence satire, try 'Ivan Kudovbin' in Michael Frayn's *The Original Michael Frayn* (London: Methuen, 1983).

Chapter 13 The card-sharp camel or 'Your number's up'

See Martin Hollis, 'More paradoxical epistemics', *Analysis*, 46.4 (1986). There are many complexities regarding common knowledge: see Chapter 23. The paradox relates to the Surprise Hanging (see *TSIF*) but appears more difficult to handle. One caveat is that maybe Camel's C means that players cannot tell who has the lower number *unless* they have 1. The text, by the way, displays more conviction than the author feels. Camel's final puzzle is akin to catch-22: see Chapter 28.

Chapter 14 Indoctrination: when believing goes wrong

Whether we can just decide to believe is raised by Pascal's Wager. Pascal argues, on a probability basis, that it is in our interests to believe in God. Even if we know which version of divinity is correct, how do we get ourselves to believe? We need exposure to believers – and hope that belief is contagious. For indoctrination, see the Open University text, revised: Nigel Warburton, *Freedom: An Introduction with Readings* (London: Routledge, 2000). Mill's free speech defence is in his *On Liberty*. Some beliefs – are they beliefs? – are impossible to live without. Try a day without accepting in any way that the past is a guide to the future.

Chapter 15 Jesters, Bertrand Russell and paradox

My Jester example follows that of Liberated Secretaries ultimately derived, apparently, from a film watched by Frank Cioffi (see *TSIF*). There are many erudite discussions of Russell's Paradox and its mathematical significance. For beginnings, see Sainsbury's *Paradoxes*.

Chapter 16 Walk on by ... ?

Ritualized humiliation occurs in Samuel Beckett's *Catastrophe*. A Charity Paradox occurs in Avishai Margalit, *The Decent Society* (Cambridge, MA: Harvard University Press, 1996). This chapter owes most to Christine Sypnowich 'Begging' in her collection, honouring G. A. Cohen, *The Egalitarian Conscience* (Oxford; OUP, 2006): she introduces Tutankhamen and Metro Man.

Chapter 17 Let the music play

Jerrold Levinson, ed., *The Oxford Handbook of Aesthetics* (Oxford: OUP, 2003) contains Stephen Davies's fine survey and the hound example. How do words apply across the senses – and when metaphorical, when literal? How similar is Oisin's psychological stress to the stress in a girder? More generally, the quest for 'something in common', when the same word is used, is challenged by Wittgenstein's 'game' example and use of 'family resemblances': see his *Philosophical Investigations*, §66ff.

Chapter 18 Time for zoological investigations – from the bedroom

Hempel's Paradox, big in the philosophy of science, leads into Nelson Goodman's 'Grue' Paradox. See *TSIF* and Sainsbury's *Paradoxes*. That science should progress by conjectures and refutations, rather than inductive support, is famously associated with Karl Popper. For background and conflict between Popper and Wittgenstein, try David Edmonds and John Eidinow's *Wittgenstein's Poker* (London: Faber, 2001).

Chapter 19 Addicted to love

For the behavioural and chemical sciences' viewpoint, see Helen Fisher, *Why We Love: The Nature and Chemistry of Romantic Love* (New York: Henry Holt, 2004). For elixir fun, try Donizetti's *L'elisir d'amore*. For philosophy, see Roger Scruton, *Sexual Desire* (London: Weidenfeld & Nicolson, 1986). The chapter casually speaks of 'concepts'; are they just certain behavioural dispositions and capabilities? Do dogs possess distinctive doggy concepts?

Chapter 20 Mercy: tempering and tampering with justice

Discussion and references are in H. Scott Hestevold, 'Justice to mercy', *Philosophy and Phenomenological Research*, 46.2 (1985). Whether atheist, agnostic or believer, we are muddled over how to handle mercy and justice – and whom to forgive. Would being God make it any easier?

Chapter 21 Speaking of whom?

Highly influential confrontations with satisfaction theories – and presentation of causal pictures – occur in Saul Kripke, *Naming and Necessity* (Oxford: Blackwell, 1980). The puzzle moves into meanings of natural kind terms and 'externalism', famously through Hilary Putnam's 'Twin Earth' examples – he of the 'Division of Linguistic Labour' – and lead to Donald Davidson's 'Swampman'. Both are explained in A. Barber's Open University text, *Language and Thought* (2005).

Chapter 22 The frog, the scorpion and 'thou shalt not'

Plato's argument, concerning gods and piety, occurs in his *Euthyphro*. A little more discussion is in my *Humanism*. Detailed papers are in Paul Helm, ed., *Divine Commands and*

Morality (Oxford: OUP, 1981). A background question is: why do you desire something? Presumably it is often because it is worthy of desire – desirable. Merely being desired is insufficient for desired objects thereby to be worthy of desire. Indeed, what we desire may not be desire-worthy.

Chapter 23 Creamy philosophers: who knows who knows ...

A frequent version, of children with muddy foreheads, apparently derives from Rabelais' *Gargantua and Pantagruel*. For common knowledge, see D. K. Lewis, *Convention* (Cambridge, MA: Harvard University Press, 1969); for comprehensive discussion, see R. Fagin *et al.*, *Reasoning about Knowledge* (Cambridge, MA: MIT Press, 2004).

Chapter 24 Exemptions: doctors, conscience and the niqab

John Stuart Mill's *On Liberty* gives the Harm Principle. For exemption discussions, try Maria Paolo Ferretti, ed., 'Rules and exemptions: the politics of difference within liberalism' in *Res Publica*, 15.3 (2009). Humanists worry about religious exemptions. Do consultants who believe abortion is murder chat easily in hospitals to those involved in such 'murder'? Regarding Campaign for Nuclear Disarmament (CND), we note that Chapter 15's Bertrand Russell was its first President in 1958. Mind you, years earlier he advocated nuclear 'first strike' against the Soviet Union. Russell would have supported John Maynard Keynes – 'When the facts change, I change my mind. What do you do, sir?'

Chapter 25 Pin dropping

Bishop Berkeley's arguments are in his *Three Dialogues* and *Principles of Human Knowledge*. Many philosophers distinguish between mind-independent and mind-dependent qualities – John Locke for one. See Jonathan Bennett, *Learning from Six Philosophers* (Oxford: OUP, 2003). Ronald Knox gave the limerick; anonymous gave the reply.

Chapter 26 Preferences: avoiding the money pump

Kenneth Arrow proved that there is no rational and fair social welfare principle for combining individuals' preferences. See Amartya K. Sen, *Collective Choice and Social Welfare* (San Francisco: Holden-Day, 1970). For rational choice, try Alfred R. Mele and Piers Rawling, eds., *The Oxford Handbook of Rationality* (Oxford: OUP, 2004). 'Ice cream choice' derived from the American philosopher Sidney Morgenbesser.

Chapter 27 A gazelle, a sloth and a chicken

The puzzle, though not the example, is Vann McGee's, 'A counter-example to *modus ponens*' in *Journal of Philosophy* (September 1985). What we commit to, when using the indefinite article – 'a' mammal – was discussed by medieval logicians such as Peter Abelard and Duns Scotus. Distinguishing between inference conditions occurs in W. E. Johnson, *Logic*, vol. II (Cambridge: CUP, 1922).

Chapter 28 On how good punishment is bad, so bad

Saul Smilansky introduces the topic. With regard to those religious believers who accept the possibility of eternal damnation, yet still behave badly – well, perhaps they rely on God's grace or divine mercy. While discussing punishment, consider the pre-punishment paradox. If authorities know that crimes will be committed, why not punish the criminals beforehand?

Chapter 29 A knowing god knows how much?

See Nicholas Everitt, *The Non Existence of God* (London: Routledge, 2004). That there cannot be a stable set of *all* truths – any infinite number of truths expands infinitely into yet more truths – is argued in Patrick Grim, *The Incomplete Universe* (Cambridge, MA: MIT Press, 1991). For humorous reflections on God's attributes, try Michael Frayn (see Chapter 12's notes).

Chapter 30 A whole cloud of philosophy – from cogito ergo sum to a drop of grammar

Wittgenstein's quotation is from his *Philosophical Investigations*, part II, §xi. For introduction, see P. M. S. Hacker, *The Great Philosophers: Ludwig Wittgenstein* (London: Orion, 1997). For biographical interest, try Rush Rhees, ed., *Ludwig Wittgenstein: Personal Recollections* (Oxford: Blackwell, 1981). Complexities arise once we focus on how surroundings determine what our thoughts are about: see Chapter 21's notes for Barber.

Chapter 31 Infinity, infinities and Hilbert's Hotel

For history and paradoxes, see A. W. Moore, *The Infinite*, 2nd ed. (London: Routledge, 2001). Many paradoxes arise when 'infinite' is applied to the world. For a small variety, see my *TSIF*. For larger, try José Amado Benardete, *Infinity: An Essay in Metaphysics* (Oxford: Clarendon, 1964).

Chapter 32 Life without end: too much of a good thing?

This piece owes much to A. W. Moore, 'Williams, Nietzsche, and the meaninglessness of Immortality', *Mind*, 115.48 (2006).

The recent debate was initiated by Bernard Williams, 'The Makropulos case: reflections on the tedium of immortality' in *Problems of the Self* (Cambridge: CUP, 1973). The case is Karel Čapek's play, now a Janáček opera, which tells of E. M. eternally aged 42. Nietzsche's eternal recurrence receives mention in our Preface.

Chapter 33 Mindful of Barbarians – within and without

Nietzsche speaks of philosophers' world-weariness. Michael J. Sandel questions morality and markets in *Justice* (London: Allen Lane, 2009). Mill's higher pleasures are in his *Utilitarianism*. For many excellent observations, see John Armstrong's *In Search of Civilization* (London: Allen Lane, 2009). Lines from Cavafy's poem are revised to fit context – see his *Collected Poems* (London: Hogarth Press, 1984). Early advocacy and wonderful observations on Cavafy are by E. M. Forster. Being human, suffering losses, let us close with Rabindranath Tagore.

> *If you shed tears when you miss the sun,*
> *you also miss the stars.*

APPENDIX 3

PARADOXES AND PUZZLES:
A QUICK FINDER

This list sets out some main paradoxes by traditional names, when available, otherwise by topic or puzzling area. As paradoxes intermesh, I have listed them from both my previous books of *Perplexing Philosophy Puzzles*, **E** for *What's Wrong with Eating People?* and **R** for *Can a Robot Be Human?* This book is, of course, **L** for *Llamas*.

INDEX

References to entire chapters are in **bold**.